PRINCIPLES OF URBAN SOCIOLOGY

James Hill Parker
Long Island University
The Brooklyn Center

UNIVERSITY
PRESS OF
AMERICA

Copyright © 1982 by

University Press of America, Inc.

P.O. Box 19101, Washington, D.C. 20036

Printed in the United States of America

ISBN (Perfect): 0-8191-2360-9
ISBN   (Cloth): 0-8191-2359-5

Library of Congress Catalog Card Number: 81-43477

To my father, Donald Parker,

and my mother, Theo Parker,

who taught me how to

think and work.

TABLE OF CONTENTS

Page

PREFACE xiii

CHAPTER ONE
The Origin and Evolution of Cities . . 3

   Origins 3
      Agricultural Surplus Theory
      Trading Theory
      Social Organization Theory

   Evolution 6
      Uni-Linear Evolutionary Theory
      Multi-Linear Evolutionary Theory
      Global Theory
      Modern School
         Energy Hypothesis
         Functional Differentiation
         or Complexity Hypothesis
         Other "World" Urban Trends

   FOOTNOTES 13

CHAPTER TWO
Demographic Theories 17

   Population Size 17
      Functional Differentiation Hypothesis
      Malthus' Theory
      Demographic Transition Model
      Heterogeneity Model

   Population Composition 21
      Melting Pot Model
      Pluralism Model
      Assimilation Model
      Conflict Model
      Cultural Breakdown Model
      Heterogeneity Source of Innovation

   Migration 27
      Push Theory

Page

Pull Theory
Transportation Theory
Technological Theory of Urban Migration

Location Theory   30
    Historical Accident Theory
    Break in Transportation Theory
    Transportation Theory
    Natural Resources Theory
    Christaller's Central Place Theory
    Access to Population Theory
    Metropolitan Dominance Theory
    Market Area Theory

FOOTNOTES   35

CHAPTER THREE
    Ecological Theories   39

    Underlying Urban Processes   .   .   .   39
        Neo-Orthodox School
        Socio-Cultural School
        Orthodox Chicago School

    Spacial Patterns   44
        Concentric Zone Theory
        Sector Theory
        Multiple-Nuclei Theory
        Combined Model Sub-Center Theory
        Spacial Distribution of Pathology

    Spacial-Temporal Patterns   .   .   .   53
        Daily and Weekly Patterns -
        Ecological Theory

    Long-term Moving Patterns   .   .   .   55
        Upward Mobility Phenomena
        Group Movement of Population
        Adjacent Neighborhood Phenomena
        Centrifugal Movement Pattern
        Wave Theory
        Invasion, Dominance, and Succession
        Hypothesis
            Tipping Point
            Declining Property Value Theory

FOOTNOTES   63

CHAPTER FOUR   Page
  The Structural-Functional Approach   .   .   67

    Systems Model   68
      Boundaries
      Feedback Mechanism

    Social Systems Analysis   70
      Pattern Variables
      Folk-Urban Continuum
      Gemeinschaft
      Gesellschaft
      Mechanical Solidarity
      Organic Solidarity
      Primary Group
      Secondary Group
      Durkheim's Formulation

    Institutional Analysis   76
      Urban Family Model
      Post Industrial Society
      Educational Institutions
      Political Institutions
      Military Institutions
      Urbanismic-Complexity Hypothesis
      Legal Institutions
      Urbanism-Rationalization Hypothesis
      Voluntary Associations Model
      Decline of Primary Groups

    Role Analysis   83
      Role Theory
      Simmel's Theory
      Impersonality in Role Relationships
      Specificity
      Role Conflict
      Status Symbols
      Formal Social Control
      Informal Drift Hypothesis

    Power Structure   92

    Status Systems   93
      Status Inconsistency
      Urbanization-Status Inconsistence Hypothesis

    Social Class   95
      Stratification and Urbanization Theories
      Multidimensional Approach

vii

Marxist Theory
Functional Theory
Functional Stratification Theory
Laissez Faire Capitalistic Theory
 of Supply and Demand

Mass Society Theory   100
    Structural and Social-Psychological
    Mass Communication
    Mass Demand
    Mass Politics
    Two-Step Flow of Communication
    Mass Organization
    Mass Movements
    Mass Entertainment

Functionalism   106
    Dysfunctions
    Urbanization-Functional Differentiation
     Hypothesis
    Latent Functions
    Folk-Urban Continuum

Dysfunctions   110
    Dysfunctions in Urban Societies
    Hypothesis of Urban Depravity
    Urban Decline Hypothesis
    Urbanization-Crime Hypothesis
    Urbanization-Civil Disorder Hypothesis
    Urganization-Ecological Crisis Hypothesis
    Urbanization-Mental Illness Hypothesis
    Urbanization-Family Breakdown Hypothesis
    Urbanization-Alienation Hypothesis
    Culture of Poverty Hypothesis

FOOTNOTES   117

CHAPTER FIVE
    The Social-Psychological Approach   .   .   131

    Mass Society Model of Urban Structure   .   131
    Bureaucratic Personality   131
        Tradition-Directed Personality
        Inner-Directed Personality
        Other Directed Personality
        Autonomous Personality
        Anomic (alienated) Individual
        Urban (civilized) man

Meaning Breakdown Hypothesis
Cultural Relativism

FOOTNOTES   137

CHAPTER SIX
The Cultural Approach   141

Within City Differences   141
    Mass Society Model
    Democratization of Life Styles Hypothesis
    Homogeneity Theory of Natural Areas

Between City Differences   145
    Cultural Diversity Hypothesis
    Ethnic Size Hypothesis
    Occupational Distribution-Cultural
    Diversity Hypothesis

Cultural Approach   146
    Cultural Change
    Urbanization-Social Change Hypothesis
    Cultural Lag Theory
    Closure Hypothesis

FOOTNOTES   151

CHAPTER SEVEN
The Conflict Approach   157

Marxian Theory of Class Conflict   .   .   157
Freudian Theory   158
Simmel's Theory   158
Psychological Approach Model   .   .   .   159
Encounter Group Model   160
Behaviour Modification Model   .   .   .   160

FOOTNOTES   163

CHAPTER EIGHT
The Future City (Planning Models)   .   .   167
    Laissez Faire or Organic Model
    Limited Use Model
    High Density and Low Density Models
    Garden City Model
    Urban Renewal Model

New Town Model
Hostile Environment Model

FOOTNOTES 171

CHAPTER NINE
Application of Principles to Urban Problems   175

  Social Systems Integration and Urban Problems   175

  Urban Growth Patterns and
  Urban Problems 176

  Size and Urban Problems 177

  Social Class and Urban Problems . . 178

  Institutional Change and
  Urban Problems 179

  Mass Society Model and
  Urban Problems 179

  Population Size and Urban Problems . . 181

  Population Composition and
  Urban Problems 182

  Spatial-Temporal Patterns
  and Urban Problems 182

  Location Theory and
  Urban Problems 183

  Migration Patterns and
  Urban Problems 184

  Theories of Conflict and
  Urban Problems 185

  Power Systems and
  Urban Problems 187

  Complexity, Social Class, and
  Urban Problems 188

  Functional Analysis and
  Urban Problems 191

	Page
Technology and Urban Problems . . .	192
Evolution and Urban Problems . . .	192
The Folk-Urban Continuum and Urban Roles	193
Bureaucratic Roles and Urban Problems	195
Life Styles and Urban Problems	196
Urban Personality and Urban Problems	197
FOOTNOTES	199
APPENDIX	203
ABOUT THE AUTHOR	209

xi

P R E F A C E

Urban sociology texts often tend to be tedious expositions of all known facts about modern societies. Little attempt is made to focus on urbanization and its consequent effects in a systematic way. One searches in vain for a systematic presentation of theory. This text on the contrary, will attempt to systematically organize theory and research that are uniquely urban. Alternative theoretical perspectives will be compared and some research evidence presented. Whenever possible theories will be integrated with one another. In this way theory will be organized to be maximally beneficial to both the beginning student and advanced researcher.

This text will not attempt the impossible task of dealing with all the theory in urban sociology or reviewing all the voluminous literature on the subject. Only the most significant theory and research will be presented, in keeping with our objective of parsimony and simplicity. Hopefully the result will be a sharpened appreciation of the theoretical issues and thrust of research activity in urban sociology.

The book will be organized around the variable of urbanization. To the extent that urban sociology is a subdiscipline it must have a focus of its own and the basic focus is the phenomena of urbanization itself.

In its most parsimonious expression it refers to degrees of population size and density. There are a number of reasons for viewing urbanization in this way. First, most government statistics are based on this definition. Of course, this in and of itself would not be sufficient reason to adopt it. Perhaps, more important, this is a conceptually clear definition when it is connected to complex, social organizational and cultural outcomes of population concentration. As long as urbanization is conceived of as a social organization and cultural variable, as well as a population variable, clarity can be brought to the sub-discipline of urban sociology. There is precedent in sociology for treating urbanization in

this way since a number of investigators, either explicitly or implicitly, treat urbanization as a "population" variable as well as a social and cultural variable. Finally, a focus on urbanization (as defined
here) reduces urban sociology to manageable proportions.

It is entirely possible to look at the
field of urban sociology from many different viewpoints.
Many investigators have preferred to look at urbanism
as something a great deal more complex than mere
numbers or social density of a region. The city (or
urbanism) is often described in terms of its social
structure, its unique culture, its interdependence
with a hinterland, and the complexity and heterogeneity
of life styles. It is true, of course, that the city
can be described in all these terms and differentiated
to that extent--from folk, primitive and peasant cultures. It is quite clear, for example, that what we
call cities involve an extremely complex social structure. Here we find a wide variety of roles, to varying extents, interdependent with one another. We find
a fine interweaving of economic systems with educational systems, and educational systems with family, political, and legal systems. We could hardly describe the
educational system of New York City without referring
to the plethora of legal restrictions and bureaucratic
rules. Neither could we describe this educational
system without referring to finely graded status and
power systems which exist both within and outside of
the school. An educational decision in this city involving who goes to what school involves a whole host
of issues which have little bearing on education, per
se, but nevertheless, must be dealt with. Questions
arise about racial balance, whether busing of students
should be allowed, the kind of programs that should be
available to the student, and a host of subsidiary
questions.

In the same way we can see the complexity
of social structure of an urban region with almost any
superficially simple problem. Take, for example, the
problem of police protection and the public's reaction
to it. In the public mind, a crime wave exists in New
York City. Nearly every person feels in some way personally endangered by the possibility of violent as-
sault, robbery, or some other form of criminal act.
The police authorities representing the police and
legal system of the city are subject to a number of
pressures from both within and without their organiza-

tions. Somehow public opinion must be manipulated to assure the public that something is being done about the crime problem, or that the problem is not as great as it appears on the surface. To this end, the police make use of another institutional means, the mass media, to "cool out" the public reaction, or to publicize its effectiveness. !The interpenetration of social systems does not stop here, however. Often the police is subject to conflicting pressures from the community which puts excessive demand upon the resources available to the police. The business community, for example, may see the protection of their business establishments as having the greatest priority and put pressure on the police at this end. At the same time, property owners and neighborhood groups may demand an excessive measure of protection. Somehow the police and legal authorities must balance these conflicting claims for police protection. To make things even more complicated, there are often organizational pressures within the police department and legal agencies. Several issues within the New York City police department, for example, have surfaced within the past few years which indicate the complexity of this single urban institution.

First of all, enormous problems were created when it became evident that there was widespread corruption within the police department itself. How to deal with this, or even whether or not to admit it to its fullest extent, became problems of monumental proportions.

A second complex, interorganizational problems, involved the replacement of uniformed policemen holding desk jobs with non-uniformed civilian workers. The difficulty in solving this problem of vested interests, (on the part of uniformed policemen) is still being worked out.

A third interorganizational problem, which indicate the organizational complexity of urban institutions and social systems, involves the hiring of "female" policemen. Here, women's rights organizations put enough pressure on the police department and city government to admit the hiring of policewomen to patrol the streets with male counterparts. Needless to say, there were many complaints from (jealous) wives, policemen and others, that such a system would not work.

We have merely scratched the surface with our few examples of the complex interweaving of social

xv

systems and institutions in urban life, but perhaps we have indicated to some extent the kind of complexity of social organizations of urban societies and some of the basis of the insistence of some urban sociologist that urbanism is much more than a matter of numbers.

Other urban sociologists have also pointed out that the hallmark of urban civilization, or the city, is the diversity of cultures and life styles. In the city, many ethnic, religious, and other sub-cultures interact affecting one another to one degree or another. In New York City, for example, we perhaps find the epitome of cultural diversity and the development of unique life styles. It has been estimated that there are close to a million homosexuals in the metropolitan area alone. Together with these we find a variety of women's action groups, ethnic leagues, various protest groups, and a plethora of special-interest groups. For almost any kind of person there is a group ready-made for him in the city, if he can find it. The history of cities shows this same diversity of cultures, classes and life-styles. Ancient Rome, large cities in the Near East, and the European cities during the middle ages, were composed of a wide diversity of people. At the very least, the rise of cities has always produced a class structure with different class levels and within these class levels, sub-classes based on occupational specialization.

It has also been pointed out that a true urban civilization develops a high culture which is not a characteristic of agrarian, peasant or folk cultures. The city, in its most developed form, has been the seat of high cultures, involving, at different times and places, elaborate religious pagentry, music, literature, and other forms of the arts.

All these cultural and social structural characteristics, then, have been pointed out as being the real essence of urbanism, not mere numbers alone.

By defining urbanization, in terms of population density and numbers, we initially leave out all the richness and variety of urban life we have just described. However, although we do not discard these cultural definitions of what urbanism is, we will find, as we progress through this book, that size and density of population almost invariable bring forth these cultural and social structural characteristics of city life. We have no quarrel with those that prefer the

cultural definition of urbanism, for it is valuable and
informative. However, we find that seeing urbanism as
basically stemming from the size and density of population, is a more parsimonious and systematic way to begin, at least, to talk about urbanism.

There are many ways to organize and classify theory in urban sociology. We could center our
discussion around one particular theory and make it
serve as the focal point of our discussion of all urban
sociology. This indeed would be a viable and integrated way to approach the subject. If nothing else, it
would constitute a single strand around with which to
weave, contrast and compare various other points of
view. A second way we could approach urban sociology
would be to attempt to integrate most or all of the
theories in the field. This would be difficult, if not
impossible, at this point, since such wide divergences
in framework, terminology and assumptions, separate
each theoretical point of view. The third way which
we have chosen seems most feasible at this point, given
the general disarray of sociological theory and, especially, urban theory. This third alternative can be
called the eclectic approach, where theories are chosen
which seem to elucidate certain kinds of problems better
than other theories. Not only is our approach eclec-
tic--choosing the theory to fit a particular type of
problem-- but, in general, these theories we have chosen are of the middle range, as described by Robert
Merton, nor are they too restricted to minute problems
or on the level of grand theory, which attempts to
create the very broadest framework. Instead we have
chosen to focus on those middle-range theories which
have some grounding in empirical research or could
easily be tested by extant empirical methods. Our
eclectic approach is not entirely composed of discrete theories, however, for we attempt, whenever possible, to relate one theory to another, either to
compare them or contrast them. Throughout the book we
will attempt to integrate theoretical orientations
whenever possible. Finally, we will attempt through
our eclectic approach, to criticize the shortcomings
of each theory and, conversely, to bring out the most
useful aspects of each theory.

In order to provide maximum continuity from
chapter to chapter, an attempt will be made to show
how the preceeding chapter is related to the next one.
In short, we are attempting an eclectic, middle-range
theoretical approach to urban sociology, with an eye

on integrating and criticizing the various approaches.

CHAPTER ONE

The Origin and Evolution of Cities

C H A P T E R   O N E

The Origin and Evolution of Cities

As Durkheim has pointed out in his <u>Elementary Forms of Religious Life</u>, it is easier to grasp the underlying principles of a social phenomena by looking at its most simple or elementary forms. In his study of religion he chose to study primitive religion and, especially, animism. This same principle probably holds true for the study of urbanism as a social form, where we can begin most efficiently and easily by studying the early forms of city life. In these early forms we can detect some of the underlying factors that made the city evolve as a social form and delineate some of its primary dimensions. Also, by tracing some of the early evolution of the city, we can see additional factors that consistently came to play an important part in the evolution of cities in general. Some of these fundamental factors from which early cities sprung forth, continue to be part of the basic defining attributes of city life. We will find that the division of labor or specialization has always, from the beginning, played an important part in the evolution of the city. Likewise, dependence upon trading with a rural or peasant hinterland has always had an important function. This brief history of the origin and evolution of cities, then, provides us with a baseline to gauge and evaluate further developments in urban life. Indeed we will find that some of these early trends are still operating, such as the increasing division of labor, the increasing use of non-human energy resources, and the general growth of population.

Origins

The city, as a social form, has been in existence for roughly 6,000 years. The earliest cities developed in Mesopotamia, with other urban civilizations developing soon after in the Nile and Indus Valleys. Much later, urban civilization appeared in Central America. All of these early cities had several things in common. Among them were a form of settled agriculture, a new form of social organization that was directed by an elite, generally of a military or priestly class, and a natural environment that provided a surplus of food. It is widely held that the crucial factor in all of these cases was the development of settled agriculture that provided a surplus of food to support specialists in secondary occupations, forming the expertise necessary for the successful development of city life. This theory may be called the Agricultural Surplus Theory of the origin of cities.[1] Evidence for this theory has been the occurrence of this factor in every early development of city life, but more importantly was the inherent logic of such an argument based on very simple observations. The logic appears to be as follows. Without specialization, city life is impossible. The only way a society can support specialists is to produce a surplus in basic economic activity. Since the basic economic activity at the dawn of city life was agriculture, city origins must have occurred as a result of an agricultural surplus. Jacobs has questioned a number of these assumptions on the basis of some recent archeological findings in the Near East. We may call her theory the Trading Theory.[2] She questions whether a surplus is necessary to produce specialists, in fact, she suggests that specialists are the ones who produced the surplus. Specialists, she contends, produced the articles that were used for trading purposes which in turn was the basis for urban development. The trading of seed and livestock, in particular, led to new, improved strains and provided the basis for an agricultural revolution. Although her argument is quite involved, she reconstructs the archeological evidence in this way. The trading and wide dissemination of seeds and livestock created a wide variety of types. People consciously or unconsciously kept the seeds and livestock that was most productive, thus, improving the various strains. The outcome of this trading and wide dissemination of different types resulted, eventually, in a surplus of food. An interesting sidelight of her theory stresses that it was in the newly developing urban areas (actually large villages) that the improvement in agriculture took place, due to trading--not in the outlying agricultural areas which were somewhat more isolated. The second trading economy in this particular urban area under study apparently revolved around the trading of flint and obsidian, with the flint coming from outlying areas and the urban food surplus coming from the newly formed cities. Only later, according to Jacobs, did the new improved agricultural

4

strains become adopted in the outlying areas. It is
obvious, however, that although Jacobs contends that
trading was paramount in the origin of cities, (at
least in the Near East) some food surplus was necessary to begin the process of city building. This is
true, apparently, even though trading was supposedly
the basis of the development of new agricultural
strains.

Thus, she contends that the agricultural
revolution came after the development of cities and a
trading economy. If anything, surplus came about as
a result of trading and specialization, not vice versa.
At present, it is difficult to evaluate this theory,
since it is based mainly upon one piece of field
research. It does suggest, however, that a simple
agricultural surplus theory may not be adequate to
explain such a complex phenomenon. At the least,
Jacobs' theory raises the question of whether there
might have been more than one source of surplus and
whether fairly complex social innovation (such as
trading and specialization) were necessary before the
agricultural revolution occurred. Some theorists have
suggested such a Social Organization Theory.[3]

It has been suggested that four or five
separate innovations, including those in social organization, were necessary in all areas of the world
where cities developed. First of all, of course, it
is suggested that a food surplus was necessary to
support the new urban population. Secondly, it has
been suggested that new forms of political organizations had to be developed, often centering around a
priestly or military class, which served to organize
the construction of public works--especially irriga-
tion projects, distribution of food and other goods,
and the defense of the city. In a sense it is suggested that city life necessitated the development of
social stratification and political institutions.

Further, specialization of occupation
developed within the cities to provide trading goods
to exchange for agricultural goods to support city
residents. This, in turn, involved some system of
transportation to facilitate trade--usually through
the use of animal power or sailing vessels. Social
Organization Theory, however, emphasizes the changes
in social structure that was necessary to develop true
cities.

5

Nevertheless, it is apparent that agricultural innovation was roughly concomitant with the rise of cities, as were certain technological and social innovations. Just how important each was to the origin of cities has yet to be determined. The surplus theorists may have confused concomitant variation with causality. It may well be the case that both agricultural innovation and social and technological changes were factors in the rise of cities.

Evolution

The evolution of cities thereafter presents an equally perplexing problem. Although some theorists question whether one can usefully employ an evolutionary perspective, it does seem useful to ask whether there is any pattern in the development of urban societies.

Uni-Linear Evolutionary Theory had its beginnings with Henry Lewis Morgan.[4] The theory was basically that social evolution always occurred in the same sequence among all societies in a series of stages. According to Morgan, the stage of savagery was followed by that of barbarism, and in turn by civilization. Monogamous family structure followed polygamous family structure; settled agriculture followed nomadism, et cetera. Others, including Taylor, continued working along these general lines.[5] It became increasingly obvious that such a global and simple formulation was not supported by ethnographic data. These sequences simply did not always, or even usually, occur.

Anthropologists found hunting-gathering peoples who, for example, practiced monogamy, others which practiced polygamy, and still others which had other marital arrangements. They found that hunting-gathering peoples could have a developed political system or little formal political system at all. They found communist societies among various cultures with different economic bases, and various forms of religion within cultures with similar economic and family systems. Furthermore, it became clear that cultural development did not form a nice step-wise progression from one predetermined form to another. Evidence of cultural borrowing from one group to another further complicated the picture.

In reaction to the excesses of linear evo-

6

lutionists, anti-evolutionist thought culminated in the
school of Franz Boas which explicitly rejected any form
of evolutionary theory and focused instead upon careful
ethnographic data collection and description.[6]

A resurgence of interest in evolutionary
theory in the thirties and forties brought about several new developments. One of these was <u>Multi-Linear
Evolutionary Theory.</u>[7] Basically this theoretical perspective held that there was more than one course of
evolution in human societies; that there may be many
paths of development. This perspective maintained that
the sequence of development of any culture could take a
variety of paths, and that there was no "set" pattern
that must emerge. Hunting-gathering people might
evolve into settled agricultural people, or nomadic
herding groups. Monotheistic religions might well
evolve into polytheistic religions.

Also emerging was a <u>Global Theory</u> which
focused upon the over-all trends in "world culture" and
contended that cultural trends must be seen in the context of the whole world not just in discrete societies.[8]
Global Theory looked at the world as a whole, including
all societies and cultures and contended that by looking at world civilization as a whole, certain evolutionary tendencies or patterns could be detected. Certainly, they found many exceptions to these general evolutionary patterns, but they believed that a number of
general trends, especially related to urbanism, could
be detected taking a world-wide perspective. It seemed
to them that the long-term view yield emerging characteristics of world cultural evolution that examination
of discrete, individual cultures could not reveal.

Look at it in this way--certain general
trends could be discovered. There have been criticisms
of this perspective centering upon the idea of "world
culture." Critics maintained that such a concept had
no meaning. They further emphasized that world culture
does not exist nor is there a process of development
throughout the world. Only individual cultures exist
and most processes of change occur only within these
cultures.

The criticism, of course, is increasingly
inaccurate with the growth of international trade,
travel, technology, financing, and government. There
does, on the contrary, seem to be emerging a "world
culture" which is shared by a large proportion of the

7

world's peoples.

A third new perspective which we may call the <u>modern school</u>, has combined all the previous ones mentioned and appears to be a compromise among them. This perspective assumed that most culture change was multi-linear, taking many different directions. However, a "world culture" perspective could be adopted with respect to any uni-linear evolutionary trends that exist. Certain "world culture" trends were described which appeared to be uni-linear. Among these trends was the steady growth in energy consumption described by White in his <u>energy hypothesis</u>.[9] Stated simply, this theory contends that social evolution in the world at large involves the steady increase in energy utilization, although it is obvious that there have been individual cultures where this did not occur. He traces the use of energy throughout the world since the beginning of recorded history and finds a more or less steady increment in the amount of energy used by many societies in the world. At first human and, somewhat later, animal power was used. This provided very little horsepower for each person in a society. Later sailing vessels, water power, and windmills augmented man's supply of power. About the time of the industrial revolution steam power was developed from the burning of coal and wood. Still later electricity was generated from coal and oil. With the advent of the train and the internal combustion engine still more energy was available. In our own time enormous amounts of energy may be tapped through the use of atomic energy and hydrogen fusion.

Another trend was described by Parsons in his <u>functional differentiation</u> or <u>complexity hypothesis</u>.[10] He finds, after looking at world culture as a whole, that there has been a gradual increase in role specialization, and therefore, complexity of social organization. Again he does not assume that this is true of all individual cultures or that this is the most important trend in the evolution of world culture.

What Parsons is saying is that throughout the world over the ages we have been building more complex social structures. Instead of a few occupational specializations as we find in many preliterate cultures, we now find thousands of occupations within modern societies. Not only has the division of labor become more complex as urbanization has increased but the development of specialized institutional forms have also evolved. In modern societies we have, among others,

8

clearly defined political, economic, legal, educational and other institutions. These institutions are further subdivided into specialized sub-institutions. Within the economic institutions, for example, we have systems that deal primarily with finance, others with production of goods and services, and those that deal exclusively with retail and wholesaling. Even these could be further broken down into sub-specialties. Specialization has not always been so evident in the world. As the world has become more urbanized, specialization has increased accordingly, until now our society consists of a vast array of roles, interrelated and interdependent with one another. It is doubtful, as Parsons suggests, that cities as we know them could be possible without this proliferation of role specialization. Thus, one of the primary world culture evolutionary trends has been directly related to the growth of cities. Not only do we find a drastic increase in role specialization, institutional specialization, and subspecialization, we also find that cities themselves often have specializations such as New York City as a world entrepot. Entire regions, or even countries, often specialize in particular products or services, carrying the process of differentiation and specialization even further.

These latter two theories are certainly very limited in comparison with the early evolutionist formulations, but they do seem to avoid the main excesses of uni-linear evolution while retaining the ideas in limited form that they proposed.

A number of other "world" urban trends might also be noted, although they have not been explored systematically. Among them, of course, is the process of urbanization itself. The growth of cities and the urbanization of the world has been increasing gradually since the origin of cities.

The growth of cities over the past several thousand years has been in the nature of an exponential curve. Very little of the world's population was urbanized until about 1800 A.D. Since that time the proportion of people living in urban areas has steadily increased until in 1970 many countries of the world, including the United States and Western Europe had 70% or more of their population urbanized. At the present time Asian countries are also rapidly becoming urbanized, with nearly 100 cities in the world with over 1,000,000 population. It is entirely conceivable that in another fifty years most of the world's population will live in cities of 100,000 or more.

Other trends associated with urbanization might be the growth of technology, the growth of larger political units, and the growth of population in general.

Population also has increased at an exponential rate during the last several hundred years. For many thousands of years the population of the world remained fairly stable, increasing by only slow increments. With the advent of the industrial revolution in Europe and later in other countries, the combination of high (traditional) birth rate and improved medical care, produced what has been called a "population explosion." Some countries are doubling their population every twenty to thirty years, especially in the "underdeveloped" areas of the world. Other countries which have reached a high rate of urbanization and industrialization have leveled off in their population growth. Nevertheless, one of the "world trends" has been the exponential increase in population, and much of this increase has been absorbed in the cities. It is clear that, to accommodate the drastic increase in population, many new and large cities will have to be built during the next fifty years.

There has also been a world evolutionary trend toward greater use of sophisticated technology, aside from the pure increase in the use of non-human power. Starting from fire, the wheel, and other rudimentary technologies, many have evolved highly complex electronic, machine, and transportation technology. If we define technology as the ability to transform the "natural" world, man has dramatically increased his ability to do so over the ages.

We have discussed in this section, some basic ideas that underlie a more complete discussion of urbanization which will be undertaken later on. We have pointed out the utility of defining urbanism in terms of size and density of population as a simplifying model to begin with. It has become obvious, however, that city life involves much more than this, and that other sociologists have pointed out that there are cultural patterns that are indigenous to city life, and that specialization and complexity of social organization ought to be considered in any definition of what constitutes a city.

Our discussion of the origins of cities makes this latter point very clear. Early cities were not just larger population aggregations than their village predecessors, but also evolved complex social patterns of stratification, specialization and power. They certainly depended upon a surplus of food, or an agricultural revolution to evolve into cities, and they had to develop trading patterns between cities and with hinterlands to complete their evolution. This short history of cities at least in terms of their origin, make it clear that cities involve and have always involved more than just population density. It is only for begining with a simplified model that we chose to see the size and population density as a basic urban variable and a basic characteristic defining cities. There is obviously room for argument along these lines as to what, indeed, constitutes a city and makes up what we call today "city life."

Our further explorations into the further evolution of cities underscores this point. If indeed we call talk about the "evolution of cities" or of culture in general, it involves more than just the increase and density of population aggregations. We have suggested that the evolution of cities involve (worldwide) a drastic increase in specialization of roles, institutions, and other elements of social organization. We have further suggested that the pure complexity of organization has developed along with the evolution of cities. Also without the increase in energy production and consumption it is very doubtful that urbanism as it exists today, would have developed. Finally, the growth of sophisticated technology has developed throughout the world and in large measure has made wide-scale urbanization possible.

With this brief introduction, we will proceed to the examination of one of these crucial variables in the development of cities, perhaps the basic one, demographic or population variables and theories explaining them and their relation to urbanization.

11

F O O T N O T E S

[1]Gideon Sjoberg, "The Origin and Evolution of Cities," Scientific American (September, 1965), pp. 41-53.

[2]Jane Jacobs, The Economy of Cities (New York: Vintage, 1969).

[3]Robert Adams, "The Origin of Cities," Scientific American (September, 1960), pp. 153-168.

[4]Lewis H. Morgan, Ancient Society (Chicago: Charles Kerr and Company, 1877).

[5]Edward B. Tylor, Religion in Primitive Culture (New York: Harper and Row, 1958).

[6]Franz Boas, Race, Language and Culture (New York: Free Press, 1940).

[7]Julian H. Steward, Theory of Culture Change: The Methodology of Multilinear Evolution (Urbana: University of Illinois Press, 1963).

[8]Robert Redfield, "The Folk Society," American Journal of Sociology, 52 (January, 1947), pp. 293-308. See also "Tepoztlan: A Mexican Village (1930) and The Little Community (1955), Gideon Sjoberg, The Preindustrial City (Glencoe, Illinois: The Free Press, 1960).

[9]Leslie A. White, The Evolution of Culture (New York: McGraw-Hill, 1959).

[10]Talcott Parsons, Societies: Evolutionary and Comparative Perspectives (Englewood Cliffs, New Jersey: Prentice Hall, Inc., 1966).

C H A P T E R   T W O

Demographic Theories

C H A P T E R   T W O

Demographic   Theories

Since one of the basic characteristics of
cities and urbanization in general is the growth of
population, it seems wise at this point to focus upon
the relation of population to city structure and growth.
Although, as we have pointed out population size as a
minimal characteristic of cities, it is nevertheless a
very important one. It is related to such other city
characteristics as specialization, differentiation of
institutions, and, eventually, the physical structure
of the city itself. With these points in mind, our
focus will be upon the primary importance of both the
size and characteristics of populations as they effect
city growth and development.

Population Size

One of the basic constraints on the development and growth of cities is the size of the population.
It is well known for example that societies that have
either a declining population or an excessively fast
growing population are likely to experience slower economic growth.

Of even more basic interest is the limits
placed on specialization by a small population base.
In short, urbanization with its attendant specialization of roles cannot develop if the size of the population is too small. The number need not be terribly
large, however, as evidenced by the extensive city
building and specialization that has occurred throughout history with a population base of less than ten
thousand. This functional differentiation hypothesis
also implies a certain density as well as size as a
prerequisite for city building. That is, ten thousand
people spread out over fifty square miles might not be
sufficient for city building, whereas five thousand
within a two mile radius might be sufficient. Density
seems to be necessary to insure adequate access between

17

persons who have complimentary specializations. Adequate size insures some of the prerequisites of specialization, namely a wide range of abilities and interests, and a sufficient market for specialized products and services.

Access between persons with complimentary specializations is increased by population density, especially in large cities, because many specialists live or work within a small radius.

For example, in large cities there are jewelry sections of the city that contain many different jewelry specialists who do very specialized work for one another, or sell rare or unusual items to one another. Other sections of large cities have antique centers where hundreds of antique stores deal with each other in rare goods, provide markets for one another, repair services, and international marketing services. This list of specialized sections of the city could be expanded almost indefinitely. In a word, cities, such as New York, London, or Paris, specialization and the cooperation of specialization reaches its highest peak to such an extent that virtually any item can be bought, exchanged or repaired in a given center of the city. We are suggesting that, as a city grows, complimentary specializations grow, and as a result a vast interdependence of specialization results. Since certain specialties require a very large "market area," such as antique jewelry, only very large cities provide the market area sizable enough to support their businesses and specializations.

The question of how large an urban population group might become was first answered (unsatisfactorily) by Thomas Malthus. He maintained that population growth is mainly limited by the resources available. He argued that people will reproduce until there are no more resources (especially food) to support additional population. At this point people will begin to die from inadequate diet and disease. The only other conceivable limits to population growth according to Malthus' Theory are moral restraint and war. Neither are very effective. We have witnessed urban cultures (e.g. Ireland, France) that have declining or stable populations yet they have not reached the limits of their resources. Thus Malthus seems to have been at least partially wrong.

Under the social and economic conditions

existing at the time Malthus was writing, his reasoning made perfect sense. Indeed the tendency for the birth rate to increase faster than the food supply was endemic. He was also correct in observing that the only natural ways to restrict populations was death through war and disease, or starvation. He did mention "moral" restraint in child production but apparently had very little faith in its efficacy.

Since his time, new techniques including the effects or urbanization itself have had the effect of rendering his theory and predictions incorrect. A useful model showing the discrepancies in his theory appearing since his time, linking the population size with urbanization in particular is the demographic transition model.

This theory states that as populations go through different stages of urbanization, the balance between death rates and birth rates changes, thus changing the rate of population growth. In the first stage of low urbanization, cultures have very high birth rates and very high death rates, thus producing a relatively stable population size. The second stage of moderate urbanization causes the death rate to go down radically due to better health practices and medical technology. However, the birth rates remain the same as in less developed societies thus resulting in a very high rate of population growth. The third stage is ushered in when a culture becomes very highly urbanized, as in the case in the United States. In this stage, death rates remain low, but birth rates begin to drop drastically. In time the two rates assume a rough balance and population size remains stable and may even go down. If this is true, which it seems to be, the real remaining questions are: 1) will we enter the third stage fast enough to avert a world-wide population crisis and, 2) why is it that people decide and carry out the desire to have fewer children in highly urbanized cultures?[1]

The first question is still unanswered but it appears as if we may suffer a world-wide population crisis before population stabilizes. Projections of population growth in the third world clearly indicate a crisis situation in some countries before the year 2000. Even in the United States of America population growth remains a problem and has not yet stabilized. The answer to the second question is still a series of partically researched hypotheses. One hypothesis is that it becomes economically unwise to have many children in an urban culture. Children usually do no useful work in cities yet they require a great deal of investment. With social insurance and the breakdown of the extended family, they are no longer useful as support in one's old age. The second major hypothesis is that improved birth control methods, especially the pill, allow people to restrict their family size easily. The evidence for these two hypotheses is mostly circumstantial and inferential. For example, it is clearly the case that children are not an economic asset in the city, in fact, they are an economic liability. Also, it is clear that the use of artificial birth control methods is increasing, especially among urban dwellers. Whether these are the real or most important reasons for the drop in birth rate, has still not been established.

Although already referred to as tangentially, population size has another important relationship to urbanization. Other things being equal, ceteris paribus, the greater the size of the population of an area the greater the variability in characteristics of the population. This has important implications for the development of functional differentiation as we have already mentioned, but it also has important effects on social relations, innovation practices, and culture change, which we will discuss later. This model is best described as the Heterogeneity Model. Just why this principle exists is rather complex, but several major reasons can be given. The first reason is a statistical one; namely, that the larger the sample of most populations, the greater the probability that extreme cases will be encountered. The second reason is a result of migration. That is, when a population grows, normally, growth is due to in-migration from other population groups, to some extent. To the degree that these contributing populations are culturally different, in-migrants will contribute new variability to the absorbing population. The third major reason is social. As people of different cultural backgrounds interact in an urban setting the probability of new social or cultural forms evolving is a function of the degree of variability to begin with. Thus a highly heterogeneous population will produce more new social forms than a homogeneous population given the same level of interaction, and other things being equal. Here we have an interaction effect; heterogeneity produces more heterogeneity. At some point, however, synthesis and integration may take over and the variability begins to be reduced.

Population Composition

Now let us look at the effects of population composition or urban social processes.[2] The aspect of composition we wish to consider here is the degree of heterogeneity of cultural and social characteristics. One important effect of heterogeneous populations are the social processes by which diverse elements of the population come to adjust to one another, when styles of life are in conflict or are contradictory. One outcome may be called the Melting Pot Model.

In this situation the various groups coalesce to form a new and unique culture to which each individual group brings its contribution. The end result is not a number of separate cultures but a monolithic one. Each cultural group gives up some of its heritage and acculturates some new elements from other cultures. A second outcome is what is called the Pluralism Model, which is best exemplified perhaps in Switzerland. In this country each culture (e.g. French, German, Italian) maintains its uniqueness and lives peaceably side by side with the other. Nothing new is created, but each group by the process of accommodation manages to live and let live. A third outcome, which appears to be most characteristic of American cities, is the Assimilation Model. In this case, a dominant culture such as the WASP's of New England, gradually absorb and assimilate new groups such as Italians or French-Canadians into their dominant way of life. This requires that the new groups acculturate to a new way of life and give up their indigenous culture. At present, various groups in the United States are wavering between assimilation and pluralism. A good example might be the Black population; some of whom desire to become a part of the dominant White society, others wish to retain unique elements of their own culture and live and work in their own communities.

The assimilation model is usually seen as consisting of three generational phases. The first generation (the immigrants) generally stay within their own ethnic group, involving themselves in ethnic churches, the ethnic community in general, and do not make any great attempt at assimilation. In fact, the source of their social and psychological stability lies in their ethnic solidarity. An example of such an

21

ethnic community is the Lower East Side in Manhattan,
which for many years was a Jewish immigrant Ghetto.
Other areas in New York City have served similar purposes. There have been Black ghettos, Norwegian en-
claves, Italian neighborhoods and so forth... This
situation exists in a muted form even today, as far
away from the city center as the suburbs on Long Island,
where predominantly Jewish suburbs or Italian suburbs
are found. The studies of neighborhoods in Chicago in
the 1920's showed a similar pattern of residential segregation, particularly among first generation groups.
In the terminology of the Chicago sociologist, these
were called natural areas. They were called natural
areas because, theoretically, they evolved from the
natural process of economic and social competition for
available land and housing. Since that time, it has
been observed that it is not only similar economic
circumstances that cause ethnic groups to segregate but
other reasons involving group identity, mutual support,
and discrimination by other groups may be involved. In
retrospect, then it appears that the Chicago School
placed far too much emphasis upon economic competition
to explain the existence of residential segregation and
the evolution of "natural areas."

The second phase of the assimilation process,
occurs among the members of the second generation of a
given ethnic group. This second generation, or children of the immigrants themselves, is often caught between two cultures. They are marginal men, who are
neither basically ethnic (like their parents) nor are
they fully assimilated into the dominant culture. They
are, on one hand, socialized into their ethnic culture
by their parents and other relatives, but at the same
time are exposed to the values and culture of the wider
society. It has been observed that this marginal status
places the second generation in a particularly precari-
ous position. They appear to be vulnerable to identity
problems concerning "who they are," and often show a
high rate of delinquency and other forms of deviance,
although this varies considerably from group to group.

The third phase of assimilation, occurs
among the members of the third generation (the grand-
children of the immigrants). This third generation,
theoretically, has generally succeeded in becoming assimilated more or less fully into dominant American
culture and have cut their ties to their ethnic group,
except perhaps for minor things such as eating habits,
certain ethnic holidays and nominal recognition of

being of Polish, Jewish or some other ethnic ancestry.
Generally speaking, this third generation is extremely
anxious to be accepted fully as "Americans" and often
take some pains to avoid any hint of having any ethnic
background.

It should be pointed out that the assimilation pattern is not always this clear cut and that a
four or five generation model might be more appropriate
for some groups. For example, this author's own research into the assimination of French-Canadians indicate that a four or five generation model is more appropriate for this group. It has also been suggested that
although ethnic ties may break down in three generations,
a new form of quasi-ethnic stratification takes its
place, where people's identification centers around religious affiliation, and three major centers of social
identification evolve; namely, Protestant, Catholic,
and Jewish.

The fourth outcome is the Conflict Model.
This outcome involves a continuing battle, either physical or social, between groups who differ in their cultures. It may be that one wishes to assimilate or dominate the other, or that each wishes to destroy the
other. These conflicts may go on for a long time and
may even eventuate in the destruction of one or both
cultures. The destruction of American Indian culture
is the result of such a conflict. The gradual destruction of native American Indian culture and, in fact,
virtual genocide, is now clearly emerging as a grim
fact of American history. Not only did the non-Indian
general population systematically attempt to destroy
Indian culture, but during many periods, it was public
policy of the Bureau of Indian Affairs to break down
and destroy Indian indigenous culture. This Indian
case, however, is not primarily an urban situation,
occurring as it did in the remote and less settled parts
of the country.

Better examples can be found within the
urban centers themselves to illustrate the conflict
resolution of heterogeneity. The Chicago sociologists
in the 1920's, for example, were clearly aware of the
conflict between groups struggling for scarce resources
within Chicago. They saw each ethnic group banding
together to greater or lesser degrees to fight off or
destroy other ethnic groups who were encroaching upon
their "territories." Contemporary examples abound illus-
trating the nature of ethnic group conflict in cities.

The fighting (juvenile) gangs of the fifties and sixties
were in many cases oriented around protecting their
group's "territory" from encroachment by other ethnic
groups, often with the consent and encouragement of the
adults of the community and community leaders. Not
only were these "gangs" instrumental in protecting "territory," they were often engaged in protecting their
ethnic group from predation by other ethnic groups of
their girl friends (endogamous restrictions) and upon
personal property. Perhaps not the least of their functions was to prevent outside ethnic influences from
penetrating the community.

Another, perhaps more pertinent example of
conflict between ethnic groups in contemporary cities,
is the relations between Blacks and Whites. Although
there is some evidence of accommodation and cooperation,
the primary model for explaining Black-White relations
in cities is probably the conflict model. This conflict
shows itself in many forms and contexts, but probably
nowhere more evidently than in residential segregation
and the resistance of Whites to living next to Black
people. On one hand the Blacks are anxious to expand
their options for living areas, and on the other hand
the Whites are generally adament in their desire to
contain them in ghettos. This conflict has led to arson, restrictive covenants, personal abuse and social
shunning and ostracism. To a large extent the exodus
of Whites to the suburbs has been a desire to escape
from the expanding Black neighborhoods. This conflict
also shows itself in the fights over "busing' Black
children to predominantly White schools, and in resistance of governments at all levels to improve the living
conditions of predominantly "Black" areas, through
better social action programs, community resources and
financing of housing and businesses in these areas.

Now let us consider certain other outcomes
of heterogeneity. One we might well call the Cultural
Breakdown Model. With competing cultures and life
styles existing and interacting within the same city,
people are continually confronted by other explanations
of the world and values to live by. In short, their
own traditional world views are brought into question.
In a melting pot society this is especially severe,
since attempts at maintaining cultural uniqueness have
been largely abandoned. The more traditional views are
questioned, the weaker they became until they may break
down completely. Until a new ideology is developed and
adopted, widespread confusion concerning proper belief

and behavior may result. This condition has been variously discussed by sociologists as anomie, alienation and meaninglessness. Let us just expand for a moment the relation of moral breakdown to the development of the division of labor and heterogeneity in urban society.

Durkheim, the famous sociologist, called this a societal condition of anomie, which roughly translated means a breakdown in the norms of the society. His argument was restricted mainly to the effects of the division of labor and specialization. He maintained that as a modern, industrial, and urban society developed the social "glue" that held the society together changed and that people were held together by mutual interdependence of each other's roles. Under these conditions, the old source of social norms and solidarity had a tendency to break down since people no longer agreed upon norms and values. As norms and values became increasingly undefinable by the individual, personal and social pathology was often the result. In a capsulated form he was saying that complicated urban societies produce moral breakdown which in turn results in pathology. It may be argued that it is more than the division of labor and specialization that creates this breakdown (indeed if it exists). It may be also that the presence of so many different idea systems and styles of life throw many people into confusion regarding norms and values. That the complexity of urban life itself breeds anomie.

A more positive result of heterogeneity may occur, however, and often does. There is a great deal of evidence that creativity and innovation is largely an urban phenomenon. One only has to think of a city like New York City to find examples of the creative effects of a heterogenous society. This city breeds new social movements, new ventures in business and technology, new experiments in intergroup relations, and is the center of the creative arts. The city is continually grappling to solve racial, environmental, and other problems that precede the efforts of other parts of the country. The reason for this is no doubt complex, but at least one factor is that of heterogeneity of cultural forms of life styles. The more variety that exists in a society the more the likelihood that innovation will occur. This might be called the Heterogeneity Source of Innovation. The reason for this effect is probably a result of having more elements of culture to combine and secondly having a vacuum of cultural meaning brought about by urbanization and thus creating a climate for

the adoption of new cultural forms. The evidence for
this theory is not systematic but rather consists of
observations that "great civilizations" tended to occur
at the cross-roads of trade where many cultural influences combined and interacted. One only has to think
of Ancient Judea, Greece, and Rome to furnish examples
of such a phenomenon.

We have already referred to the vast creativity and innovation that emanate out of cities like
New York, but the list could continue to a much greater
length including Tokyo, Buenos Aires, Amsterdam, et
cetera. A look at the history of art is instructive as
an example of the creative potential of cities that are
at the center of the world trade. When the Greeks
controlled the Mediterranean, their art and philosophy
flourished. When the Romans occupied the center of the
world trade, the development of new social and governmental forms flourished. Later, when the Arabs controlled Mediterranean trade and constituted a cross-
roads of cultural influences, their art and science
flourished. We could continue this analogy by pointing
to the succession of world trade centers that, in turn,
became cultural and artistic centers. In order, the
list would include the Italian cities, the Dutch and
the English.

In this section we have tried to point out
the effects of size and other population characteristics
on the nature and functioning of the city. Clearly,
size in and of itself, is an important prerequisite for
the development of a city. Beyond this, urbanization
itself seems to have important effects on the population
growth of the people in that city. We have found that
as urbanization increases, the birth rate tends to level
off and come into some kind of balance with the death
rate. To this extent, urbanization diminishes population
growth and the threat of a "population explosion." Size
is also related to the variety of cultures and life
styles found in the city. As a city becomes larger,
generally, variations in group life and heterogeneity
become greater. This increase in heterogeneity has a
variety of implications for any city. First of all, the
different cultural and ethnic groups must come to some
accommodation with one another and we have pointed out
that this may result in the development in very different processes including the melting pot process, where
a new culture is created, the assimilation process,
where over three or more generations the ethnic group
becomes assimilated into the dominant culture. And

26

finally, we have seen that conflict between different ethnic (and religious) groups may be basic modes of adaptation or interaction between these groups. Population and population characteristics, then constitute very basic considerations in the understanding of how a city functions.

Migration

Our next consideration also involves population, but in this case we are primarily interested in the movement of population as it exists in cities and the effect it has upon city life.

America, for many centuries, was an agrarian society, in which the vast majority of the people lived on farms or in small villages. It was through the vast migration of peoples from these areas and outside the United States that provided the population of the newly developing cities. It is our purpose here to examine some of the reasons for this migration, some of its patterns, and some of its consequences for urban life. Again, we are dealing with the variable, population, but in a somewhat different sense.

Another important effect of population on urbanization stems from the migration of population. Urban centers have always been a magnet for population movement. The reasons for this are, partly, a function of the urban centers drawing power as a source of livelihood, protection, and a cultural milieu of freedom. In the middle ages and soon after, cities were citadels where landless serfs could establish their freedom, begin new occupations, and where entrepreneurs could operate in a favorable climate for business. For the last two thousand years there has been a steady flow of people into urban areas with the greatest influx being within the past fifty years. The flow has been so great that many technologically advanced countries, including our own, the large majority of the population is urbanized. There are several theories which attempt to account for this rapid influx into the cities.[3] The first theory is called the Push Theory of migration. This accounts for migration by calling attention to all the forces in a person's immediate environment that pushes him out of an area. Forces that have been considered include persecution, economic disasters, general lack of jobs, natural disasters, and over-population.

Perhaps the most prominent reason is lack of job opportunities in the present place of residence, and a greater opportunity for employment in another. People may be drawn to big cities because of the cultural or ethnic discrimination in areas from which they came. In the South, for example, many Blacks moved North to avoid the blatant racial discrimination that they were forced to submit to in there. Dislocations in the economy in different parts of the country including the shutting down of plants, the drying up of mineral resources, and the general depopulation and lack of opportunity in small towns, are also factors in many cases. The climate for some people is a motivating force for moving. The climate may be too hot, too cold, too dry, or too humid, and adversely, affect people, especially with severe medical problems. It might be pointed out that many people have moved to Arizona and New Mexico, to avoid the high humidity of other parts of the country that aggravates rheumatoidal conditions. In some cases it may be possible that people move to avoid relatives and associates that have come to make life unpleasant for them. Lastly, perhaps, is the pure fact of boredom and the desire for new experience. People may move to get "out of the rut," to see new places, and get a new start. It is obvious that there are many potential reasons that people elect to move away, and we have only touched upon a few of them.

There is, however, another important set of forces which act upon the individual to cause him to move. These series of forces comprise what we call the Pull Theory of immigration. Forces involved here include economic opportunities, social opportunities, relatives, friends (living there) and climate. Again, there is ample evidence that these forces do account for some of the migration to the cities. However, for a more or less complete theory of migration, both the push and the pull theories must be combined.

The pushes and pulls are, to some extent, additive and when the pushes and pulls outweigh the inducements to stay, the person will generally move. Apparently, during the past several hundred years the inducements to move to the city have generally outweighed counter-inducements to stay in the rural areas. If one had to choose one most important "pull" it would have to be economic inducements. Migration studies, indeed, show this to be a powerful force causing people to move to cities.

In a dynamic changing society such as our own, business failures, product changes, and business relocations are a common occurrance. In most cases the companies involved make little attempt to relocate or provide new jobs for their displaced employees. In such cases, the individual himself must uproot his family and move to an area that does provided employment. In many cases the only "booming" areas are large urban centers that are drawing in new industry. Economic inducements, of course, may be of a more positive kind, where the individual has a job in his old residence, but sees greater opportunity for making money in another place. In most cases it is the large metropolitan areas that offer the highest wages and chances for advancement. There are, of course, cases in which entire regions, or towns become economically depressed such as Appalachia, where the flow of new immigrants for economic reasons becomes a steady stream to cities like Chicago.

A specification of the above theories is the Transportation Theory of migration. This states that the flow of migration generally follows the least expensive and most efficient transportation routes, all other things being equal. An example of this might be the heavy migration from the South of Blacks to Washington and Baltimore, following well-established and relatively short routes from the deep South. These "traditional" migration routes also include migration from Appalachia to Chicago and other cities in the Midwest, migration from the South up the Mississippi to Chicago, migration from Canada to New England's textile cities, and migration from Puerto Rico to New York City. The net effect of these traditional routes is to "load up" certain cities with poor in-migrants who require resocialization, social services, and in some cases, additional social control in terms of police protection and intervention. These "terminal" cities for migrants, of which New York and Chicago are good examples, suffer all the negative consequences of having to deal with poor, untrained, and in many cases dependent people. The welfare loads, the school problems, and probably the crime rates all reflect the negative consequences of this in these cities.

Another specification of the push-pull theory is the Technological Theory of Urban Migration. This theory explains the rapid growth of cities and migration to cities in terms of technological innovation. The rise of scientific and mechanized agriculture is certainly one major reason for the decline in the farm population during the past century and constitutes a "push" out of rural areas and into cities. On the other hand, technological developments in the cities led to the rise of manufacturing and consequently, the enlargement of job opportunities in urban areas, thus constituting a "pull" toward the cities.

Again, we have been talking about "population" as a basic variable in the study of urban sociology. This time, however, we have focused upon the movement of people into the cities, the patterns they have followed, some of the reasons they moved, and some of the repercussions for the cities themselves. Through this entire section, population has been the focus of our attention as it is related to the city life, its size, its characteristics and its movements.

Our next section will deal, again, with population and the city, but now our focus will be upon why population grows in certain places to form cities and in other cases areas fail to develop cities in their region. The whole question here again is demographic or having to do with the relation of population to the development of cities.

Location Theory

The influence of demographic variables on urbanization is further elaborated around what is commonly called Location Theory, although it is more properly a set of theories only loosely articulated with one another, attempting to explain why cities are located where they are.[4]

The first location theory which perhaps accounts for the fewest cases, is the Historical Accident Theory. This theory states that sometimes at the whim of a military commander or more commonly, a political leader, a site is chosen for a garrison, fort, or capital. As a result of this decision, a city grows up in this spot. Many cities in Europe, for example, were formerly garrisons or forts. There are also examples of Capitals becoming a large city because of political decisions; for example, Washington, D. C., and Brasilia, Brazil. It may well be that the first explorers, tradesmen, or settlers happened to pick that particular location. It has been noted that many deep-

water ports were located in less advantageous sites than
nearby locations afforded. At the present time the
degree of influence of historical accident is probably
underestimated due to the difficulty in identifying
this factor as a definite influence. A more important
factor according to many urbanologists is outlined in
the Break in Transportation Theory. The theory states
that the cities tend to grow up at points where two
different types of transportation systems meet and cargo has to be transferred from one transportation system
to another. A city grows up purportedly because ware-
houses have to be built, housing is established to house
transportation workers and longshoremen, and facilities
have to be provided where cartage can be broken into
different units most suitable for the new form of transportation. Thus, the re-packing and transfer of cargo
provides the economic base of the new city. There are
certainly, examples of such cities. Chicago, probably
is a good example, at least in its early days when it
straddled the Chicago River, linking the Great Lakes
and the Mississippi River and also was a central rail-
terminal for the Midwest.

        A related theory of location is the Trans-
portation Theory. This theory simply states that cities
are likely to be located near transportation routes,
especially near water transportation. The fact that
many of the world's great cities are located either on
the ocean, large lakes, or rivers, gives credence to
this theory. It is also very common for large cities
to be located at the confluence of two bodies of water,
such as the junction of great rivers and ocean harbors.

        The Natural Resources Theory states that
cities are likely to be located near a natural resource
since it reduces transportation costs in moving raw
material and finished products. Examples of these kinds
of cities are mining centers such as Denver, and agricultural service cities such as Des Moines. Often, with
the exhaustion of the natural resources, these cities
shrink to a shadow of their former size, or in some
cases, disappear altogether. Obvious examples of this
are "ghost towns" in the western part of the United
States that were formerly thriving mining centers.

        The most highly developed type of location
theory is Christaller's Central Place Theory.[5] This
theory states that cities are located near the center
of a hinterland, which serves as a market area and a
source of raw materials, especially if it is farmland.

In a relatively uniform geographical area with similar
characteristics (e.g. rich farmland) cities will be
spaced out in a symmetrical fashion providing each urban
area with a hinterland commensurate with its size and
specialization. This theory seems to fit best when
dealing with uniform geographical areas with a farming
economic base. When the topography varies or the economic base varies, his model does not fit as well.

Probably connected with the symmetrical
nature of market areas found by Christaller is Zipf's
rank size rule, which observes that there is a pyramidal
distribution of cities of different sizes.[6] There being
only one New York metropolitan area, but many cities of
25,000-50,000.

Also probably connected with Christaller's
observations is another location theory, namely, the
Access to Population Theory. This predicts not only the
location of cities, but their size and position relative
to each other, to a great extent. This seems to stem
from the necessity of a city of any given size to have
a market large enough to support itself, and being somewhat outside of the market area of competing cities of
various sizes. Bogue has elaborated and tested such a
perspective in his Metropolitan Dominance Theory.[7] His
general thesis is that large metropolitan areas exercise
constraints on its hinterland in terms of the kinds of
economic activities they can engage in. In short, a
symbiotic relationship exists between dominant (metropolitan) areas and sub-dominant outlying areas. Thus
the existence of already existing population areas determine to some extent the possibility of establishing
new urban centers.

It should be pointed out that Bogue defines
the metropolitan area (as do most sociologists) much
broader than the area enclosed just by the city limits.
He includes the suburbs surrounding the city, and con-
tiguously built-up areas extending from the city. For
example, the New York Metropolitan Area includes not
only the five boroughs, but also Eastern New Jersey and
Southern Connecticut, as well as the suburbs on Long
Island, Westchester County, et cetera. Another example
of a metropolitan area might be Chicago which includes
not only the corporate city limits, but the contiguous
built-up areas around it extending into Southern Indiana,
and reaching up to Wisconsin. The concept of Metropolitan Area, therefore, attempts to group population into
interdependent contiguous areas regardless of legal city,

county, or state lines.

A criticism might be made of Bogue's model
of metropolitan dominance at this point. He stresses
the hierarchy of dominance beginning with large metropolitan areas and eventually reaching the relatively
dependent and powerless towns and villages. It might
be pointed out that the dominance works two ways. For
example, the City of New York depends upon a vast market
area reaching out hundreds and even thousands of miles,
composed of smaller cities and the people in them who
buy the goods and services of New York City and thus
sustain it. The use of metropolitan centers as central
market areas constitutes a two-way form of dependence.
On the one hand the more dominant (larger) center may
determine the kinds of economic activity lesser areas
may engage in, but in turn, these lesser areas support
the economic activities of the metropolitan area.

All three of these above mentioned theories
point to a general theory which has yet to be developed,
which for want of a better term could be called the
Market Area Theory. This theory should be applicable to
at least capitalistic societies. Briefly, the theory
implies that a city of any given size requires an adequate market area for its goods and services. Generally,
the bigger the urban area, the larger the market area
required. Furthermore, each city must compete against
other urban areas for markets, and in the process the
number of large, medium, and small cities within a given
area are limited to the few that survive (in the competition). Cities in a given area as a result of competition form a hierarchy and a system of dominance and
sub-dominance, with the larger cities probably taking
the most lucrative products, services, and markets. As
a result of this process, a more or less spatially
symmetrical pattern of cities occurs, along with a pyramidal distribution of cities according to size.

We could, perhaps, more profitably, look at
the entire "Megalopolis" as a primary dominant market
area. When we say megalopolis, we mean long stretches
of built-up areas that reach for hundreds of miles. One
of these megalopolises is the Eastern stretch, reaching
from Portsmouth, New Hampshire to Washington, District
of Columbia. Some have made the area a little shorter
(from Boston to Washington) and called it Boswash. Another megalopolis stretches along the Great Lakes region,
including Chicago, Detroit and Cleveland. Some envisage
this megalopolis eventually stretching all the way to

33

Albany, New York. This same megalopolis is often said
to include parts of Canada, including Toronto. A third
megalopolis stretches along the West coast including
San Francisco, San Diego, and Los Angeles, California.
A fourth is developing along the gulf coast, especially
in Texas, which includes Dallas, Fort Worth, and Hous-
ton. A fifth may be developing in Florida, linking up
various cities in that state, along the coast. So areas
of dominance may be becoming these great, extensive megalopolises which stretch for hundreds of miles, even
crossing national boundaries. It may well be that the
fundamental urban unit in the future, and perhaps at the
present time, are these huge stretches of built-up areas
called megalopolises. Bogue, in short, may have unduly
restricted his areas of dominance to metropolitan areas,
rather than these units.

This section, dealing with the location of
different sized cities, has cited many theories. These
theories can all be lumped together as "location theories." The trouble with all of these approaches is that
no one of them, explains by itself, the location of all
cities. Different cities appear to require different
reasons for their location or a combination of reasons.
Again, we have to look at individual cities and decide
which model to adopt rather than to select one or several
theories that explain all. We have pointed out some of
the inadequacies of these theories including Bogue's
theory of metropolitan dominance. We might add that
these explanations all turn out to explain city location "after the fact" in sort of a post hoc fashion.
We look at the city, such as Chicago, and then make up
reasons or apply theories to account for its location.

In any case, this section has continued our
interest in population as a variable in explaining and
understanding cities. This time, however, we restricted
ourselves to those theories which dealt with the reasons
for the particular location of cities. We asked ourselves the question, "why is Chicago, or New York, or
Podunk, Iowa, located where they are?" Why isn't Chicago or a city like it located fifty miles to the West,
or why isn't New York City located in New Jersey or
Maryland which have excellent harbors? It is clear we
have not arrived at a single, simple model to explain
this, however, perhaps we have suggested some relevant
reasons, or interesting variables.

F O O T N O T E S

[1] For a discussion of this see J. Bogue, "The End of the Population Explosion," The Public Interest, No. 7, (Spring), pp. 11-20.

[2] For a discussion of these processes see Milton Gordon, Assimilation in American Life, (New York: Oxford University Press, 1964).

[3] For a discussion of this see Everett S. Lee, "A Theory of Migration," Demography, 3:1, pp. 47-57.

[4] A good discussion of these location theories can be found in Ralph Thomlinson, Population Dynamics (New York: Random House, 1965), pp. 281-288.

[5] Walter Christaller, Central Places in Southern Germany (Englewood Cliffs, New Jersey: Prentice-Hall, 1966).

[6] George K. Zipf, Human Behaviour and the Principle of Least Effort (Cambridge, Massachusetts: Addison-Wesley, 1949).

[7] Donald Bogue, The Structure of the Metropolitan Community: A Study of Dominance and Subdominance (Ann Arbor, Michigan: University of Michigan Press, 1949).

CHAPTER   THREE

Ecological Theories

C H A P T E R   T H R E E

Ecological Theories

In this next section we conclude our interest in population as a main variable in explaining the development and nature of city life. This time, however, we will focus our attention on the distribution of population "within" cities. Here, we will be interested in such questions as "why does a city grow along certain directions, or "why is the population distributed the way it is within a given city, or all cities?" This general topic has been the focal interest of human ecologists for some time (although not the only one), and it is in this area of human ecology, as a branch of sociology, that we will be concerned with here. We will look for patterns of growth, patterns of movement, and patterns of segregation of population within the city. Again, we may not be able to come up with a definitive answer but at least we may be able to indicate some alternative ways of looking at these patterns and processes. So now we proceed our continued interest in population as a variable, but this time with population as it is distributed within the city.

Underlying Urban Processes

The spacial distribution of various functions and cultural groupings within cities has fascinated human ecologists for some time.

The first approach, historically, was the Orthodox Natural Area approach. A natural area was, according to Park and his students, an area of the city where people of similar social backgrounds resided as a result of competition for space. It was not implied by Park that people of similar cultural backgrounds got together because of preference or affinity, but rather were forced by "economic" circumstances to do so.[1]

Park distinguished between cultural and biotic levels of organization. It was the biotic struggle for space based on competition that determined the spacial location of people, in large part. The cultural

39

level based on communication and consensus was seen as a superstructure resting on the biotic level, and secondary in importance.[2] Park's students delineated and studied several of these "natural areas" in Chicago such as "the Gold Coast," "Hobohemia," and "the Slum," during the 1920's and 1930's.[3] The principle of dominance was used to explain the creation of natural areas and the general ecolcgical pattern of the city. Those groups (i.e. ethnic groups, industries, professions, et cetera) who successfully competed for space came to have a position of dominance in a given area, and tended to displace other competitors for the land. Industry and business in particular were the most successful in competing for space, thus setting the main outlines and boundaries of land use. Other users fitted into and competed for the remaining space. Since the best location for business was the part of the city with the greatest access to population, the center of the city was pre-empted by them. With any shift in population or transportation patterns, land values changed, and natural areas shifted. The "zone of transition" was essentially an area shifting from one dominant use (i.e. residential) to another (i.e. business). Park's model substantially ignored cultural determinants of land use and population distribution, and relied heavily upon a purely economic explanation.[4] It was precisely the economic determinism in his argument that provided his critics with grounds for rejecting or altering his model.

Perhaps the position closest to Park is the model of the Neo-Orthodox School which is concerned with the social organization of urban populations. Social organization, according to Hawley,[5] is primarily the way a population organizes itself for survival in a particular habitat. In short, he seems to be saying that spacial patterns are social organizational responses to economic forces rather than reactions to economic forces directly.

Hawley goes beyond a purely economic model, and asserts that social organization, whether it be groups, institutions, political parties, or ethnic groups intervene in the economic process. Another way to put this is to say that people act as interest groups or pressure groups to gain access to bits of land, or that they are drawn by group affiliation toward certain areas. This, of course, implies that social forces distort or change the direct competition of the market place. It is also a more collective view of the social process determining land use. As Hawley says, populations "organize themselves" for survival. They do not act alone as individuals, each making separate decisions, but organize in multi-faceted ways to cope with the problem of survival, and in the process affect the distribution of population in cities.

An operationalization of this perspective is contained in some of Duncan's work,[6] where he plots the clustering of different occupational groups according to zones and sectors and attempts to explain the results in social organizational terms. For example, he finds a tendency for social distance between groups to be expressed in terms of physical distance. He also finds groups at the extreme ends of the occupational prestige scale to be the most segregated. In other words, the neo-orthodox ecologists interpose an intervening variable, social organization, between economic variables and spacial distribution.

The socio-cultural school at an extreme end of the scale puts the maximum emphasis on cultural factors in determining the clustering of different types of people within the city. Firey,[7] for example, shows that elite residences on Beacon Hill in Boston cannot be explained by economic variables. Beacon Hill is surrounded by deteriorating neighborhoods and in some respects is located in an undesirable area. Firey explains the phenomenon in terms of cultural and historical values. The elite live on Beacon Hill because it is a culturally valued and historically important area. The important point that he is trying to make is that the primary value of the land on Beacon Hill is cultural not economic, per se. If, for example, all the rich and affluent people moved off the Hill, it would probably become just another piece of slum property. Perhaps a better way to state the case is to say that the value of a piece of property is not necessarily determined by its location, but sometimes it is determined by the "kind" of people that occupy that territory. If the lowlands surrounding Beacon Hill had been historically (and still were) occupied, by the elite, it too, might command a high price and be a prestigious place to live. He is suggesting, it may not be the "position" within the city that lends value to it, but the kind of people who have and do live around it. We are all familiar with the phrase "a good neighborhood," or "a prestigious address." This implies that there are certain "culturally and historically" prestigious places to live and certain undesirable places to live, regardless of their position within the city, or their value for alternative uses.

41

We have tried to establish a continuum on
which to place the various ecological schools. The
primary dimension used was economic vs. socio-cultural
determinants of land use. At one end of the scale are
economic criteria and at the other end, socio-cultural
criteria.

The middle point of this scale would be a
combination of economic and socio-cultural determinants
of land use which is best expressed by the Neo-orthodox
School of Hawley and Duncan which we have discussed.
We could make even finer divisions of this scale, having
10 or 20 points on the scale representing various proportions of economic determinants and socio-cultural
determinants. For example, we could add one point on
the scale where economics account for only one fourth
of the variation in land use, and another point on the
scale where economics account for three-fourths of the
variation. We could make this even more sophisticated
by showing that the point of the "scale" varies over
time. The "Gold Coast" in Chicago in the 1920's, for
example, may have been determined as, perhaps, three
fourths by socio-cultural determinants. Today it has
shifted its position on the scale to, perhaps, three-
fourths economically determined. It may be, then, that
the determinants of land use, not only vary from place
to place, but may also change over time.

The choice of an appropriate model seems to
depend partly on the degree of urbanization. It appears
that economic factors are more important with a low
degree of urbanization, whereas socio-cultural factors
weigh more heavily when we are dealing with a high degree
of urbanization. This might be called the urbanization-
spacial distribution hypothesis. The distribution of
population in pre-industrial and industrial cities is
an example of this hypothesis. In pre-industrial cities,
the elites were constrained to live near the center of
cities for primarily economic reasons. Not only was the
center of the city more safe from attack, but poor communication technology made it essential to live near
trade and decision-making centers. In industrial cities,
these constraints were removed, and elites were free to
move to less congested areas away from the center, basing
their location decisions to a great extent on non-economic criteria.

Today, we find in industrial societies,
especially in the large metropolitan centers, the poor
and powerless concentrated in the "inner city." They

42

are anxious to get out and move to the suburbs outside
the city where there are fewer social problems, green
grass and all the rest of the advantages of suburban
living. The middle class, by and large, already occupy
the suburban areas surrounding the city, far from the
center of the city where worse social problems abound.
They are not anxious for the "poor" and, especially,
the Black to move out there with them.

This has been a product of ecological organization stemming from the industrial revolution in the
1700's and 1800's, when the poor were forced to live
next to the factories that were located at the city
center. As transportation became better some were able
to move out further from the center. The rich, in turn,
were able to move out, far out. We have still maintained
this pattern of population distribution, even though
transportation exists to allow the poor to move further
out. The difficulty is that the housing costs (and the
transportation costs) increase the further out one lives.
The poor, then, are condemned to live in what has been
called the "area of transition." An area which has
"cheap" rents which wait eventually conversion to more
expensive land use such as high-rise apartments (for
the rich) and office buildings.

We are suggesting that the location of the
poor and the rich in cities has undergone a revolution,
with the poor now living in the center. The reason for
this revolution has been a revolution in transportation
and communication which no longer made it essential for
the elites to live near the center of the city.

We have examined the reasons why populations
are distributed in various ways within the city, again,
focusing our attention on population as a variable. We
have looked at various theories including the Orthodox
Chicago School, the Neo-Orthodox view, and the Socio-
cultural School, and found each of them inadequate as a
total explanation of the distribution of population.
Each focuses upon a somewhat different combination of
economic and non-economic factors. We have suggested
that a scale could be constructed placing these on a
continuum. We have also suggested that different areas
would fit better on different positions on the continuum
and that the same areas (neighborhoods, et cetera) might,
over the course of time, change their position on the
continuum. That is, in one decade a neighborhood's land
use might be determined primarily by economic considerations, and ten years later determined by non-economic
or socio-cultural factors.

In the next section we will also be concerned about population in the city, but now we will be more interested in the various patterns that populations form in various cities. Several models will be presented which claim to describe the way in which cities are laid out.

Spacial Patterns

A number of theories have been proposed to describe and, to some extent, explain land use within cities. Perhaps the most famous of these formulations came out of the Chicago School in the nineteen twenties. This is the <u>Concentric Zone Theory</u>.[8] Land use was conceptualized as comprising a series of rings or zones around the center of the city, each somewhat further out from the center than the previous one.

Example follows in Figure 1a on the following page.

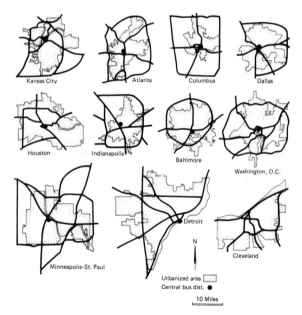

Adapted from Edgar Horwood and Ronald Boyce, <u>Studies of the Central Business District and Urban Freeway Development</u>. (Seattle: University of Washington Press, 1959.)

Figure 1

Three Theories of City Growth*

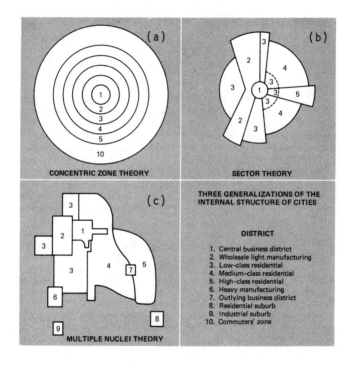

*From C. D. Harris, and Edward L. Ullman, "The Nature of Cities," The Annals, 24 (November, 1945).

The scheme illustrated on Figure 1a was mainly the result of the analysis of Chicago's land use patterns in the twenties. The first inner zone comprised
the central business district. The next zone out from
the center was labeled 'the zone of transition' in which
land use patterns were changing from low density uses
to high capitalization, high density uses. Essentially,
the land was being held by speculators for future development of the expanding central business district.
Until that time, property, like slum housing, was allowed
to deteriorate since it was not economically sound to
invest capital improvements in property that would soon
be put to different uses. The third zone was called the
area of workingmen's homes and the fourth, the zone of
middle class dwellers. Comparable to what we now call
"the suburbs" was the outermost zone labeled the com-
muter's zone.

Unfortunately, this model describes only a
few cities adequately, however, it is useful as a partial
explanation of many urban areas where there is some
approximation of this model. In all cities there can
be found a central business district especially in urban
centers established since the widespread use of auto-
mobiles. Also, there is at least some evidence of a
transitional zone around the business district of most
cities. Again, however, there are often several deteriorating areas within a large city and they are not
always in close to the central business district. Also,
there is a strong tendency in older cities for the working class to live in close to the Central Business District and the the middle classes to live farther out.
In spite of these approximations to the Concentric Zone
Theory, a full description of most cities requires the
use of additional models.

Another well-known model of city land use
is Hoyt's <u>Sector Theory</u> (see Figure 1b) which, is more
properly, a theory of urban growth patterns.[9] Nevertheless, this theory attempts to explain why different
kinds of land use are located as they are. Briefly,
his theory states that residential land use grows outward from the center of the city, not evenly around the
center but along several radii or sectors. Thus, he
finds that at the outer fringes of a "sector" new high
rent residential property is located, and as this property becomes older, lower class residents move in. The
high-rent districts, then move even further out along
the outer edges of the sector, since they are hemmed in,
literally, by lower status sectors.

Likewise, industrial areas appear to develop in sector fashion according to Hoyt, along river valleys, water routes, and railroad lines. Thus, the pattern of development, far from being uniformly concentric, is more like wedges of pie-shaped areas or tentacles of an octopus extending out from the center of the city. Again, there is some evidence that this kind of pattern commonly exists, but it does not describe or explain all land use patterns in cities.

Further, the theory does have the advantage of expanding our view of how the patterns of population in the city does vary from the simplistic concentric ring theory. It is obvious that concentric rings only roughly describe some cities, and that we can see evidence in most cities of "sectors" developing out from the center of the city. It makes good sense that such a pattern should exist. Since many transportation routes extend from the city center out to the outskirts of the city, they provide a natural nucleus for population expansion and growth. It barely needs to be pointed out that access to transportation draws population growth, so it is no accident that population should grow in sector fashion along these routes. A second reason for the development of sectors may be the existence of natural boundaries that extend from the center of the city, such as rivers, mountain ridges, and swamplands, which channel the growth of population, outward in a sector fashion. There are also social boundaries which may channel population in this fashion. For example, if a slum district has grown up extending from the center, newer and more expensive housing may avoid this area and be forced to move out sector-fashion. Perhaps, however, the best explanation of the sector pattern is the existence of transportation routes and natural boundaries.

This sector theory, however, does not exhaust the models of city patterns, that sociologists have observed.

A third theory is Harris and Ullman's Multiple-Nuclei Theory of land use[10] (see Figure 1c). This theory asserts that there are many centers of most cities, not just one. Each center specializes in some activity such as retailing, wholesaling, education, et cetera. The general explanation underlying this theory of sub-center specialization is that different specializations require different environments. Thus, heavy manufacturing requires considerable space and must be near

47

transportation lines and away from high-status housing. Retail trade must be central to population with easy access and preferably close to other retail establishments. Sometimes, however, multiple centers exist because they were formerly centers of separate towns.

There seems to be, then, two main reasons for multi-nucleated patterns. On the one hand many cities, including New York, Chicago, and Los Angeles, were originally made up of separate smaller cities. Only gradually did they draw together, with the interstitial spaces being filled in, and the whole area being incorporated as one city. These separate centers, however, continued to be sub-centers of the larger city, although more and more dominated by the larger city center.

The second main reason for sub-centers, it appears, is the specialization of certain areas centering around certain wholesaling, manufacturing, and retailing establishments. Certain parts of the city seem to be more useful for different kinds of activities and this fact is reflected in sub-center specialization.

A third reason for sub-centers might be added at this point and that is the necessity for neighborhood service and retail centers which are easily accessible to the local population. Although with the use of the automobile this becomes less necessary, people still seem to desire and support local shopping areas.

A major criticism of this multi-nuclei theory is the implication that cities may have more than one "major center." A brief survey of most cities indicate that there is only one major city center, and the other "centers" are sub-centers.

Given this fact, the theory could be better described as a Combined Model Sub-Center Theory. We could illustrate this by picturing one major center (such as mid-town Manhattan) surrounded by numerous sub-centers such as the financial district in Manhattan.

A second criticism of this theory is that there appears to be numerous levels (or a hierarchy) of sub-centers within most cities. There is the main city center, surrounded by large sub-centers, which are in turn surrounded by smaller sub-centers and so forth. This suggests a model of a number of concentric ring

48

systems within a city, many overlapping one another.

Thus, we are faced with three differing
models of land use which are obviously contradictory.
None of these models by themselves adequately describe
or explain land use. Together, however, they seem to
describe most of the patterns found in American cities.
This requires, however, an AD HOC kind of explanation
and description of each city encountered. That is,
Chicago may be largely described in terms of concentric
zones with some admixture of sector and multiple-nuclei
theories. Los Angeles, on the other hand, shows a much
more distinct multi-nucleated pattern. Besides using
these models in combination, they also seem separately
useful in describing different distributions. That is,
the distribution of apartment buildings, small families,
families with working wives, do show a concentric distribution. However, prestige of residential areas show
a sector distribution.

We might inquire at this point what the usefulness of these "spacial" theories might be for anybody.
Is it of any use to draw a series of concentric circles
to describe a city, or to divide the city into pie-
shaped pieces? Does it make any sense at all to spend
so much time and effort trying to describe the spacial
patterns of cities? The answer is an unqualified, yes,
if indeed these "models" are accurate. There are many
uses for such models and we might begin by discussing
how businessmen might use such information.

Businessmen would be very interested in
knowing the direction in which the population of a city
would be like likely to grow. By knowing this they
could plan the building of business establishments and
assess the value of property. They could also assess
the kind of services needed, the amount of housing required, and the type of housing necessary. Businessmen
are not the only ones who could profit by knowing such
things. City planners and social agencies of all kinds
could make an assessment beforehand, what kind of services to provide, how many schools to build, the highways needed and many other things. Government agencies
of all kinds could profit by knowing the evolving pattern
of population movement and composition.

From a sociological point of view, such
theories could give much valuable information on populations to organize themselves spacially. What kinds
of groups are likely to live near, together and the
directions they are likely to take in the future might

also be valuable information. But most important sociologists need to know how populations in cities organize
themselves spacially, and perhaps, why.

The Spacial Distribution of Pathology has
already been hinted at. Generally, although not always,
there is a definite tendency for social pathology to be
located toward the center of the city in the area called
the zone of transition.[11] There are significant devia-
tions from this model however, whenever there are several
zones of transition in the city, there is a spacial distribution of social pathology also. Crime, juvenile
delinquency, drug addiction, divorce, and poverty, all
show this tendency. Likewise, mental illness appears
to be much more prevalent in the zones of transition.
These, however, may well be misleading correlations since
the underlying cause of these maladies is clearly not
one's residential location, but low socio-economic status.
It just happens that poor people cluster in the zones of
transition where housing is cheap. It is not only the
inexpensive housing that draws poor people to the zone
of transition although that is, no doubt, a major reason.
Another reason is, obviously, exclusion from other areas
because of one's ethnic or racial background. The con-
tainment of Blacks in inner city ghettos is a good example of this. In other cases poor people may stay in
"poor" areas because it has become customary within the
family to live there, or because members of the extended
family live there. Other people are loath to leave familiar surroundings, where they have lived all their
lives. Given the choice of moving, perhaps to a better
but new area, they may prefer the familiar neighborhood,
poor as it may be. Others than the poor may be drawn to
the "zone of transition" or inner core of the city because
there are sub-cultures with which they can participate.
For example, drug addicts or alcoholics may be drawn to
the area for this reason. Others, such as homosexuals
and artists may not be poor but, again, are drawn to an
inner city area where a supportive subculture exists.

Perhaps at this point a critique should be
made of the theory of the zone of transition and deviance
that abounds there. First of all, it is clear that high
deviance rates can be found in other areas of the city,
sometimes a considerable distance from the zone of trans-
sition. High rates of unacceptable social behavior is
not usually restricted to this area, in fact, there may
be many high deviance areas within a large city which
are quite widely separated, spacially. The second
criticism is related to the first, and that is that dif-

50

ferent kinds of deviance and social disorganization are
often found in different places. Drug addiction may be
high in one area, whereas, broken families, or prosti-
tution may be high in different areas. In other words,
there seems to be a specialization among various areas
of the city, focusing on certain kinds of deviance and
social disorganization. Some kinds of mental illnesses,
for example, are higher in the more suburban areas of
the city than they are in the inner city. Another example might be that suicide rates are among the lowest
in inner city, Black ghettos, and are considerably higher in other areas of the city.

It has already been noted that, in some
cities, the outer edges of certain "sectors" contain the
most affluent parts of the population. In general,
there is a strong tendency in older American cities for
the more affluent to live further out from the center
of the city than working-class or poorer people. This
is partly as a result of the age of housing and its
consequent rental value in different parts of the city.
Obviously, the older housing was built closer to the
center of the city when it was small, and gradually
newer housing was built further and further out from the
center as available land had been used up further in.
In the newer, western United States cities, however, the
pattern is the reverse with the inner ones having a somewhat higher status population than the suburbs. The
explanation for this is that the housing in these new
cities is newer even in the inner zones, thus, drawing
a higher status population. Another factor might be
that there is a new trend, showing itself in the newer
cities for the affluent to live near the center, especially when the housing is good. Another factor is that
the newer cities are less likely to have an enormous
central business district, thus, making it less congested,
and perhaps more liveable. Finally it is possible that
in these newer cities the population is more evenly
spread out over the city, thus making population differences more diffused over the city.

Also, generally, land values increase toward
the center of the city, and diminish as one moves further
out. The reason for this apparently is that access to
population is greater the closer one gets to the center
of the city. Access to population is a definite advantage for many businessmen and professionals, thus, the
price of land is built up. A secondary process, once
the central business district is established, is that
access to facilities draws even more (daytime) popula-

tion to the area increasing, even more, its access to population.

By the Central Business District we refer to the inner circle of the city containing main business establishments and office buildings. In terms of the concentric zone theory, the central business district is the innermost circle.

This perspective has some important implications in understanding the development of slums, the movement of slums, and the shifting of the central business district. In a sense this theory explains a lot of population movement within the city.

First, slums are, in many cases, marginal properties which are still useful to produce income but the land is not yet valuable enough or useful enough to be converted into more expensive uses, such as for office buildings. Slums, on the edge of the central business district, are in a transitional phase then. At present they are poor housing on reasonably expensive land. Given growth to the central business district, these slums will be torn down and become a part of the central business district. In the meantime, the landlord will get what profit he can from the slums until they are converted to more expensive new uses.

Our theory also explains the movement of the central business district insofar as it is related to the movement of population. Since access to the "center" of population in the city is so important, the most central area (with respect to population) will become the most expensive land and the nucleus of the central business district. If, for any reason, the distribution of population in the metropolitan area shifts, the central business district is likely to shift also toward the "new" center of population.

We have concerned ourselves with various aspects of population in the city, including the placement of cities themselves, theories concerning the patterns that city population take, and the movement and distributions of populations in cities. Now we would like to conclude our focus on the population variable by focusing extensively upon the movement over time, and of urban populations, which we have touched briefly in the preceding paragraphs.

Spacial-Temporal Patterns

Daily and Weekly Patterns - Ecological Theo-ry has also been concerned with temporal patterns within the city.[12] That is, the distribution of people changes during the day. Many transportation problems stem from this fact. First, great numbers of people travel from their residence to places of work, and back again to home at the end of the day. The fact that many people must make this trip at about the same time creates most of urban travel congestion. The nighttime population of the Central Business District is very sparse, where-as during the day it burgeons with people. The resi-dential areas during the day are composed mainly of women, children, and old people. The non-residential areas on the contrary, are, during this period, composed largely of adult men and working women. This pattern has been cited by some as having implications for socia-lization. Since home and work areas are separate, chil-dren tend to be socialized by women. Other sociologi-cal implications of this ecological separation is that the woman tends to become the socio-emotional leader of the home, providing the continuity of living patterns when the husband is away from work. A further implica-tion is that the children are prevented from observing the work-a-day world, thus, being deprived of sociali-zation in that crucial area. The conclusion that this separation also contributes to a matriarchal family power structure has not been convincingly demonstrated.

The opposite argument would take the posi-tion that men in many societies have been away from home during the day and in some cases, for weeks, so this is not unique to cities, and certainly not to large cities. Also, it has not been convincingly demonstra-ted that the husband is that divorced from contact with his children and, indeed, may spend much time with them on his off-hours. The crucial determinant may be the occupation of the father rather than whether he lives in the city or suburbs. In some occupations, such as traveling salesmen, businessmen may be away from the home a great deal, while others may spend many hours at home. A convincing argument against the "momism"theory is that for most men working hours are considerably shorter than they were fifty or one-hundred years ago, thus possibly, they have more time to spend with their families.

Not all the flow of population is between the Central Business District and home. About half of the working population living in the suburbs, also work in the suburbs.

The reason why more people are working as well as living in the suburbs is that industry and business is beginning to relocate in these outlying areas. Part of the reason for this relocation is the fact that a large population now lives in the suburbs and must be serviced.

A second reason is that business and industry are finding it too expensive to operate within the city, and tend to relocate where land costs are lower.

A third reason for this relocation is that business and industry are finding it easier to recruit workers, especially executives, to work in the suburbs than to recruit them to work in the central city.

These new patterns of people living and working in the suburbs have implications for traffic patterns in and around the city. Since so many more people work in the suburbs, highways are needed that circle the city from suburb to suburb. This new pattern may well also put less pressure on the highways leading out from the city. At the present time, the circular highways linking suburbs are probably underdeveloped, with more money being put into arterial highways leading into the center of the city. Also there is a flow during the day and on weekends from residences to shopping areas, located throughout the urban area. The reason for this is that housewives do most of the shopping while their husbands are at work, or on weekends if they work themselves. With the development of regional "shopping centers," the necessity for long trips into the city is perhaps reduced, making the trip often an excursion to a nearby shopping center. The flow of shoppers during the day is not as critical in creating congestion since it is spread out over the entire day, every weekday. During the weekend, however, the confluence of many shoppers going to shopping areas create traffic problems. With the growth of shopping centers, though, the traffic is probably reduced since shorter distances are involved and fewer people travel for shopping purposes to the central city.

A subsidiary flow from residence to the central city and sub-centers occurs during the early evening, especially on the weekends, when people travel to centers of entertainment.

The traffic flow in this case is spread out over a considerable period of time. People tend to go into the city for entertainment and back any time from five in the afternoon to five in the morning. Most of the flow, however, takes place mainly between six and twelve in the evening on weekends.

Again, the central business district tends to fill up and the residential areas lose population. The distribution of population, then, varies during the day and from weekday to weekend in a fairly predictable way.

So, in summary, daily and weekly population movements follow a fairly predictable pattern. Understanding them, contributes to our understanding of traffic patterns and problems. The basic fact underlying this discussion and these problems is that people, for the most part, live in different places than where they work, or where they shop. Since different activities of urban dwellers take place in different locations, traffic problems are increased substantially. If, in fact, people carried on all their functions in the same area, there would be no traffic problems. This fits into our prior discussion of the patterns of population in the city, and the location of different functions.

So far we have just talked about daily or weekly population movements within the city. Now we will expand our discussion to include longer term population movements in cities.

Long-term Moving Patterns

Spacial-temporation variations in the distribution of population also, obviously, varies over long periods of time. The moving habits of populations within cities appear not to be random but take on definite patterns which to a degree can be predicted.[13] For example, there is the Upward Mobility Phenomena. This is based on the observation that ethnic and other groups, with similar life chances tend, over a period of several decades, to move upward from lower-class areas to middle-class areas. This observation is so obvious that it is seldom mentioned. Nevertheless, it is an important uniformity in population movement. However, individuals within these groups may be undergoing downward mobility. On the whole, though, groups in this country, tend to move upward in this way.

55

In the history of this country each consecutive immigrant group moved socially and ecologically (that is, to different parts of the city). The first were those of English, Scotch, or Dutch descent. They were followed by the Germans, the Irish and the Italians. More recently, Black migrants from the South, West Indians, and Puerto Ricans have constituted a new wave of immigration to the large cities, and are slowly climbing up the socio-economic ladder and are in the process of moving to higher status areas of the city.

The second model is the Group Movement of Population. Groups with similar cultures tend to move as groups to roughly the same areas. There is, therefore, a tendency for "East Side Italians," for example, to move to the "near west side." Recently, for example, large numbers of Italians moved from Brooklyn to Staten Island in New York City, more or less as a group. We have also seen group movements in New York City of Germans, Blacks and various other groups. Even at this time some suburbs around New York City are populated mainly by one ethnic group.

There is some evidence, however, that there are ethnic differences in the degree that groups tend to stay together locationally. There is some evidence that this is determined to a degree by the extent to which they are discriminated against in housing and are therefore limited in choice of neighborhood.

Some groups, such as Puerto Ricans and Blacks, probably suffer the most in their choice of neighborhood due to racial discrimination. They, therefore, are likely to move as a group to the only few new areas available. Norwegians, on the other hand, not the subject of housing discrimination, have a wide selection of neighborhoods to choose from and are thus more likely to disperse and not move so much as a group to the same neighborhood.

Another variable that certainly has some relevance is group cohesion. That is, the more cohesive the ethnic or status group, the more likely they will move to the same area of the city in close proximity of one another. It appears, for example, that Italians are more cohesive as a group than Norwegians, thus we would expect the Italians to move more frequently as a group. It is probably, also, that the Jewish population is more cohesive than some other groups and, on this account, may move as a group.

We have talked about Long-term Moving Patterns of population in the city but have failed to point out that most people in cities (or elsewhere) do not move long distances.

Another model that specifies the distance of population flow is the Adjacent Neighborhood Phenomena. Studies have shown that most moves, whether as groups or individuals, are made within fourteen blocks. Thus large jumps across the city are not common. Rather, movement to an adjacent neighborhood is the norm. The precise reason for this is unclear. Exceptions to this model occurs when discrimination in housing exists and Blacks or others are forced to move to an available area further away. A quick look at the movement of Blacks in Chicago over the years, illustrate this phenomenon.

There are a number of other patterns of population movement around the city which we have not discussed, but which have importance in understanding the structuring and functioning of the city.

Another pattern which is so obvious that it is often ignored, is the Centrifugal Movement Pattern of population in the city. Due to the pressure of population, the distribution of available space, and the growth of the business district, population moves outward from the center of the city. This movement has been incorrectly interpreted by some as evidence that the central city was dying, whereas, in fact, land values in most central cities have consistently gone up. The Sector Theory, already alluded to, specifies this pattern by suggesting that population not only moves outward but along radial sectors.

There also seems to be a centrifugal pattern in most business expension and movement. This, no doubt, is a result of business following population. There has always been the tendency for businesses to move out from the center with population movement, but recently, this tendency has increased. With the establishment of regional and neighborhood shopping and professional centers, more and more people are shopping within their own suburban area rather than making the trip to the Central Business District. The result for the Central Business District has been to slow down the growth in retail trade, and to make available its facilities for other uses. These other uses have tended to be specialized wholesale and retail services, and office space which takes advantage of the central location and access to population. Examples might be a specialized fur fashion shop which must draw from a large population, or a central banking or insurance office that serves as a communication center for its metro-wide or even nation-wide operations.

As we have discussed population movement in cities we have gone from very short term movements, such as days and weeks and the patterning during such periods. Now we would like to discuss a very long-term population movement within cities which covers decades.

A theory of population movement in metropolitan areas over long periods of time (fifty years and more), called the Wave Theory, shows great promise of describing long-term population movement.[14] The theory states that waves of population move out from the center of the city in such a way that in each of twenty zones (concentric) there is a long period when population density rises to a peak and then slowly declines to a plateau. This cycle takes approximately fifty years. The crest is highest in the inner zones and decreases thereafter. This movement coincides with the fifty-year average life of economic enterprises in the city that have been observed and may, along with gradual population growth, explain the wave phenomena. A subsidiary, but nevertheless important, concept is the analogue of the tidal wave. That is, there appears to be, at the outer edges of population growth a place where the growth "crests" in a zone of maximum rate of growth. It is also worth noting that this theory fits observations regarding the centrifugal movement of urban populations.

There are a number of criticisms of such a theory, one being that it is not clear whether the Wave Theory applies to small cities or even to medium-sized cities. The second criticism involves our previous discussion of the inadequacies of concentric circles in describing population movements. If, indeed, the concentric zone theory does not fit all or even most theories, it is doubtful whether the Wave Theory can be (completely) stated in terms of concentric zones. A more careful analysis of the data might well show that some parts of the concentric zones grow faster than others and that using concentric zones, as a mode of analysis, makes it artificially look like a zonal pattern when it is not.

The implications of this wave theory for practical problems are obvious. First, if the theory is correct, we should be able to predict the changes in land use over long periods of time. We would then, expect, that land use patterns in a zone would change every fifty years or sooner. For city planners and businessmen alike, this would be an important theory. Also, if there are "crests" at the outer edges of population growth, this could be taken into consideration in planning public and private facilities, accordingly, city planners, for example, could plan highways, schools, and public housing to accommodate this new wave of population.

Another long-term population movement, described by the early urban sociologists, also often takes decades to take place. This process has been called the Invasion, Dominance, and Succession Hypothesis.[15] This hypothesis postulates a number of stages by which one kind of population in a given area is displaced by a new "invading" population. Although the number of stages is in dispute, they seem to follow a familiar sequence. First, there is an influx of just a few members of the new group. As the number of newcomers increase, a reaction among the older residents occurs, being made up of both defensive and accepting responses. Various attempts are made by the established population to limit or halt the influx of newcomers. At times these reactions may be quite violent and hostile, including such things as arson and violent assaults. Often, however, the reaction is less obvious and includes such things as shunning and restrictive covenants. During and after such a reaction, a general influx of the invading population often occurs. This may occur anywhere within two years or a twenty year period, depending on the nature of the neighborhood. Finally, a "Tipping Point" may be reached which is usually around fifty per cent, when the neighborhood rapidly changes its composition in favor of the newcomers. When this final stage is reached succession has reached its conclusion for the time being and a new group becomes dominant in the neighborhood.

A theory closely associated with this process, may be called the Declining Property Values Theory. This theory, widely held by laymen, states that when invasion by a new group occurs, espceially Blacks, property values go down. Luigi Laurenti has tested this theory using a wide sampling of neighborhoods, and finds that property values, over the long run, go up about as frequently as they go down.[16] It appears that if old residents are panicked into selling, usually by "block busting realtors," property values are likely to decline. However, if the old residents resist the temptation to put their property up for sale immediately, property values often increase.

This same Invasion, Dominance, and Succesion model also applies, with some alteration, to non-residential land use. For example, land in the zone of transition only gradually is invaded by new uses; such as office buildings or high-rise apartment buildings. Gradually the entire zone is taken over by these new uses and the former slum uses are displaced. In some instances good residential areas are invaded by commercial establishments as well, often resulting in resistance on the part of the established property owners to having the area rezoned for business. This often happens along strips of property adjoining a major arterial highway or at major thoroughfares intersections. The invasion of higher status residents on lower income property is much less common and is seldom resisted.

A criticism of this invasion hypothesis is that it is not always possible to tell ahead of time what "new land use" or what "new group" will be the invaders. Even though it may be true that we can describe changing land use, in terms of invasion, dominance and succession, this is not as helpful as it could be if it were specified what new group will be the invaders. Sometimes it will be a lower status group (of various ethnic status) that invade, sometimes it is more affluent people in new high-rise apartments or town houses or, at other times, office buildings or business establishments invade the neighborhood. Another criticism is that the process does not always move through all the various stages. Sometimes a group "attempts" to invade but is repelled, and the process stops there. At other times invasion succeeds and a new group enters the neighborhood but the stage of dominance is never reached. Finally, even if the new group becomes dominant, it may not reach the stage of succession, where the old group is displaced. So the so-called ecological process just discussed can be subverted or stopped at any point.

The ecological perspective we have been discussing at some length has dealt with population distribution within the city some of the processes involved in changing distributions of population. This ecological section has been a logical extension of earlier sections that dealt with the importance of population in understanding urbanization and city living. In this section we have discussed various models of city growth the ways in which populations move, both long-term and short-term. The theoretical importance of this ecological perspective is that it offers some insight into population distributions and movements "within" cities. The difficulty encountered, however, is that there is no one theory that human ecology offers us to explain these processes and patterns. As it stands now, ecological theory is a patchwork of theories which, to varying extents, explain the population dynamics and distributions of a city. Many times it is necessary to use a number of theories at the same time to explain, for example, the growth patterns of the city. In other cases, such as in the Invasion, Dominance, Succession Hypothesis, we find many exceptions to it, and it is, to that extent, an inadequate hypothesis.

Now we move to another kind of theoretical orientation which is still related to population in the city, but is more interested in the organization of people into social systems. Cities are not just aggregations of people who settle in certain neighborhoods or move out of them, but are also complicated social systems and systems of social organization. Now that we have completed the most basic considerations of population, we can move to understanding how these populations are organized. It is not enough to describe aggregations of people in terms of numbers. We must also understand how these aggregations become organized and how various functions of the city get carried out through this kind of social organization.

We will now examine the perspective from a structural-functional approach.

FOOTNOTES

[1]Robert E. Park, Ernest W. Burgess, and Roderick D. McKenzie, The City (Chicago, Illinois: University of Chicago Press, 1925), pp. 1-7.

[2]Ibid., pp. 115-118.

[3]Harvey Warren Zorbaugh, The Gold Coast and The Slum (Chicago, Illinois: University of Chicago Press, 1929), Louis Wirth, The Ghetto (Chicago, Illinois: University of Chicago Press, 1928), Nels Anderson, The Hobo: The Sociology of the Homeless Man (Chicago, Illinois: University of Chicago Press, 1923).

[4]Park, Burgess, and McKenzie, op. cit., pp. 1-23.

[5]Amos Henry Hawley, Human Ecology: A Theory of Community Structure (New York: Ronald Press, 1950).

[6]Otis Dudley Duncan and Beverly Duncan, "Residential Distribution and Occupational Stratification," American Journal of Sociology, LX (March, 1955), pp. 493-503.

[7]Walter Firey, "Sentiment and Symbolism as Ecological Variables," American Sociological Review 10 (April, 1945).

[8]Ernest Burgess, "The Growth of the City," in Robert Park and Ernest Burgess, The City (op. cit.).

[9]Homer Hoyt, The Structure and Growth of Residential Neighborhoods in American Cities (Washington, District of Columbia: Federal Housing Administration, 1939).

[10]Chauncy Harris and Edward Ullman, "The Nature of Cities," Annals (November, 1945), pp. 7-17.

[11]Robert Faris and H. Warren Dunham, Mental Disorders In Urban Areas (Chicago, Illinois: University of Chicago Press, 1939), Clifford Shaw, et al,

Delinquency Areas (Chicago, Illinois: University of Chicago Press, 1942).

[12]F. Stuart Chaplin, Jr. and Pearson H. Stewart, "Population Densities Around the Clock," The American City, Vol. 68, No. 10, (October, 1953), pp. 98-99.

[13]Peter Rossi, Why Families Move: A Study In the Social Psychology of Urban Residential Mobility (New York: Free Press, 1955).

[14]Ronald R. Boyce, "The Edge of the Metropolis: The Wave Theory Analog Approach," British Columbia Geographical Series, No. 7, (1966), pp. 31-40.

[15]Robert E. Park, "Human Ecology," American Journal of Sociology, Vol. 42 (July), pp. 1-15.

[16]Luigi Laurenti, Property Values and Race (Berkely, California: University of California Press, 1960).

C H A P T E R   F O U R

The Structural-Functional Approach

C H A P T E R   F O U R

The Structural-Functional Approach

A vast body of literature has grown up concerning the social structure of the city and its functions. By social structure we mean the organization and institutional network of social relations. These are composed, for analytical purposes, of roles which in turn are merely expectations of how a person should act in any given position.

A person may have many roles, for example, that of father, church member, electrician, lodge member and husband. The list could be continued almost indefinitely. If the man works in the city he may play the role of a subway rider, a taxi-cab rider, a customer at a bank, a member of an audience at a play, or a stroller in a park.

Roles are connected together into role-sets, where persons have mutual expectations of each other. One person's obligation may be another person's right. Small groups are formed of interlocking roles as a rule, and in turn large-scale organizations are made up of systems or interlocking small groups. Social structure, then, can be seen as being made up of a great many interlocking roles. Sociologists, as a rule, do not analyze social structure by looking at persons, but by looking at the various roles that the person plays. The social structure of the city can be looked at from this point of view--that is, as an interweaving and complex structure of roles. Again, when we refer to roles, we mean the way the person is supposed to act in that position. We call the "position" a status.

Functions, as used by sociologists, are the part that various sectors of the social system plays in maintaining the functioning of that system in equilibrium.

The following methods of analyzing urban social structure include to one degree or another a functional analysis, looking at the degree to which parts of the social system are functional or dysfunctional.

Systems Model

One place perhaps to begin here is the Systems Model. This model assumes that the city is a system of interrelated parts which show all the properties
(characteristics) of systems in general, whether they
are mechanical systems, biological systems or psychological systems. One of the properties we expect to find
in any true "system" is clearly marked boundaries. Unfortunately, in terms of systems analysis, cities do not
have any clearly defined boundary, but rather have a
number of different non-contiguous boundaries. Different functions of the city have different boundaries;
such as newspaper distribution, wholesale trade, retail
trade, commuting areas, and political areas. Political
boundaries, by themselves, are very confusing, since
there are hundreds of even thousands of political units
in most large cities which overlap in jurisdiction.
Thus cities, only in a very rough sense, have boundaries
and if one wishes to analyze the city as being one system,
he has to be satisfied with dealing with only rough approximations of a system with boundaries.

A second system property that we expect to
find if a city is one system in the rigorous sense is a
feedback mechanism. Only in a very rough sense, again,
do we find feedback mechanisms analogous to mechanical
systems serving the whole city. For example, the market
system which regulates prices, supply, and demand is only
imperfectly a feedback system where information concerning supply and demand for goods and services, in part,
determine the price of them. There are obviously many
ways in which this mechanism fails to regulate properly
such as price fixing, monopoly, and inadequate information on the part of consumers. These latter factors
prevent feedback altogether or provide inaccurate information.

The democratic political system is also an
imperfect feedback system, in which periodic elections
provide feedback from the electorate concerning their
evaluation of the performance of the city government.
Again, there are many sources of error in this system,
such as fraudulent elections, and lack of information
on the part of the electorate.

Also there is multiple criteria for judging
an administration, some might emphasize fiscal economy
while others might measure it by the number of social
services it provides. Some might approve of an efficient

and stable administration, while others would encourage experimentation in government even though it migh cause some instability and inefficiency. The criteria a conservative might use, would differ from those of a liberal or a radical political type. Thus, only in a very imperfect sense can we talk about urban feedback systems.

A genuine system also requires that there be some mechanism by which the feedback received can be translated into corrective adjustments on the part of the system. In short, the system should be self corrective. Even a brief survey of city functioning should convince one that many times feedback indicates problems, such as ghettos, unemployment, congestion, et cetera, but nothing is done about it. The city simply lacks the mechanismsto take corrective action even when errors are evident. However, if one is satisfied with only approximations of systems analysis, there is some evidence of self-corrective action resulting from feedback in the nature of governmental programs which attempt in various ways to ameliorate the situation.

Finally, a true system should be integrated, with various parts contributing to the proper functioning of all the other parts in order to maintain equilibrium. Of all the criteria of systems mentioned, cities fail to meet this one the most critically. Cities appear to be only loosely integrated with no clearly central source of integration. The most clearly integrating mechanism is city government, but even here integration is only partically effective.

Disregarding the analogy of the city as one single system contains serious inadequacies, it is more useful to view it as a multitude of systems only loosely integrated and often in conflict.

In fact we might say that much of American urban society is organized to prevent systematic characteristics from developing. For example, democratic theory underlying the political system makes explicit use of "balance of powers" to prevent sectors of the system from meshing and cooperating. In short it has conflict built into it on purpose, in order, supposedly, to diffuse power. The economic system likewise is built on the assumption that individual businesses and households should be in competition rather than meshing together in order to assure maximum integration. In other words, these institutions are built on a conflict and competition model, guaranteed to prevent maximum integration of functions. In this case "disorder" is created in order to insure order. In fact, some "game theorists" have characterized the whole urban process as being many different groups playing different "games" and by different rules, thereby insuring a certain lack of integration and feedback.[1]

The newspaper may be playing an "information game" where its primary play is exposed, the largest business in town might be playing the anti-union or low-tax game, and the unions might be playing a work-slow-down game. Other groups like the League of Women Voters might be playing a kind of public-service political game. Perhaps it is misleading to call these "games." A better term for it might be tactics, strategy, or goals. In any case, the point is that different groups play by different rules thus making it difficult to achieve cooperative harmony within the city.

So far we have looked at the "systems" approach to studying the city insofar as the pure systems criteria are met. Now we will go to a slightly different type of systems analysis, dealing in particular with the social system.

Social Systems Analysis

If we view urban areas as a number of loosely integrated groups and organizations, a simplified version of Parsons' social systems analysis may be applied in urban sociology. In Parsons' view, a city would be a partial social system made up of collectivities (groups, organizations).[2] These collectivities are part of a larger social system. Thus the business sector of a given city is only a fragment of a much wider (national, regional, and international) economic sub-system. Likewise the schools in a city are an instance of a national educational sub-system. These local organizations derive their values, norms, goals, and symbolic systems from a more general (societal) cultural system. The actors in this system are individuals who have internalized norms, values, and goals of the cultural system and their performance can be analyzed in terms of roles. Groups are linked together in an exchange relationship within a city. The output of one group constitutes the input of another group. These collectivities (groups) are constrained in their activities by the boundaries of other collectivities. For example, air pollution by a factory may be curtailed by the courts, and the

school board must keep its decisions within the boundaries set by state law.

These groups and organizations, working in
concert, come to establish a very unstable equilibrium
which can very easily be upset by changes external to
the city (e.g. national or regional system changes) or
changes in the cities' local organizations.

Another application of Parsons' model to
structural urban theory is his schematic of <u>Pattern
Variables</u>.[3] The pattern variables represent five dimensions which purportedly describe all roles in any
society. They can be used to describe the <u>differences
between urban and non-urban social structure.</u> The following diagram illustrates the basic typology:

Table 1

Less Urbanized Roles	More Urbanized Roles
Affectivity	Affective Neutrality
Quality	
Particularism	Performance
Collectivity Orientation	Universalism
	Self Orientation
Diffuseness	Specificity

Thus, less urbanized roles tend to involve
more emotional expression (affectivity). They tend to
be assigned more on the basis of some quality of the
individual rather than his performance, and are per-
formed with reference to particular situations rather
than according to general rules. Also, less urbanized
roles tend to be oriented more toward group than individual goals, and are less specialized than urban roles.

Just for example, let us think of a typical
role in a pre-literate or folk society. Let us, for
convenience's sake take the role of the hunter in relation to other hunters. There is likely to be a lot
of emotion shown by this hunter toward others. He will
not treat others like numbers or members of some abstract
category. He will tend to relate to each of the other
hunters on the basis of their individual, personal

71

characteristics. The hunter will also be very much
oriented toward the welfare and norms of the group,
rather than toward his own ideosyncratic needs. The
group will come first and himself second. Also, the
hunter's relations with others will probably involve
many aspects of himself, not just his role as hunter.
He and others will relate as total human beings with
all their roles and ideosyncracies. Finally, it is
likely that the hunter will have been "given" or assigned
his role as hunter, because he is a male of a certain
age, not because he has earned the right to be a hunter.
There are, of course, variations from this ideal model,
but it gives a rough idea of how roles in folk societies
are played. We should be aware that this is a continuum
and that we must have just been giving one extreme.

Now to show the differences that urban roles
tend to have, let us give another hypothetical illustra-
tion, but here involving a "typical" urban businessman.

This businessman will be very interested in
his own welfare, probably above that of any group other
than his family. He will talk to other businessmen in
a very restricted context, talking about the business
deal at hand. He will not relate to other businessmen
as "whole" or total persons, but in a segmental way
constricted by the rather narrow set of norms that govern
business behaviour. He, no doubt, will have achieved
his position through some effort of his own, such as
earning degrees at school, taking training programs, or
working himself up through the ranks. Just being a "man"
at a certain age is not enough. His relations with other businessmen will also probably be emotionally restrained, or as
we call it, "affectively neutral." He will, in all
probability, apply general rules of behaviour to the
other person depending on what social category the other
person is in. He will have a "universalistic" set of
rules, in other words, which guide his behaviour, rather
than guiding it according to the particular characteristics of the other person he is relating to.

Parsons is not the only sociologist to see
these folk-urban differences.

A number of other sociologists have constructed similar dichotomies which express structural
differences between urban and less urbanized communities.
These can be broadly designated as a <u>Folk-Urban Conti-
nuum</u>.[4] The following figure summarizes various conceptualizations of this continuum:

Table 1

Folk-Urban Continuum

Conceptualizations[5]

Less Urban	More Urban
Gemeinschaft	Gesellschaft (Tonnies)
Mechanical Solidarity	Organic Solidarity (Durkheim)
Primary Group	Secondary Group (Cooley*)
Status	Contract (Maine)
Folk	Urban (Redfield)

*Cooley coined the term Primary Group, but Secondary Group appeared later in the literature.

Let us take these paired terms one at a time and explain them.

Gemeinschaft communities according to Tonnies are basically made up of close primary relations, where people know each other well and basically agree on community values and norms. Gesellschaft communities are more like the modern city, where relations are likely to be impersonal and contacts are more formal. Mechanical Solidarity according to Durkheim is based on common norms and values. People agree on what good and evil is, or what the goals in life should be. Common action thus results from common values and goals. Organic Solidarity according to Durkheim is characteristic of modern urban communities where people do not agree on common values and goals. There are many value systems in these communities and the "glue" that holds the urban society together is interlocking roles. People cooperate because they must depend on other people's role-playing to accomplish their own objectives. The Primary Group according to Cooley is characterized by close, frequent relations that are important in socializing the person. Usually these contacts are face-to-face contacts on a frequent basis, perhaps day-to-day. The Secondary Group as it has been treated in the literature is less important

73

to the individual insofar as his socialization is concerned. It is also more formal as a rule, meets less frequently, and the members may not even meet in a face-to-face fashion, except rarely. An example of a Secondary Group is a labor union, or a large voluntary association.

According to Sir Henry Maine, a community based on Status, relies upon personal relations and the person's position in the community to organize the group and enforce standards. A community based on Contract, on the other hand, emphasizes legal codes and legal contracts to organize and control society. Finally, Redfield's distinction between Folk and Urban communities tries to explicate the important differences between the two kinds of societies which roughly correspond to the pre-literate community and the Urban community. Folk communities are tied together by common beliefs, are cut off from other cultures, by and large, and change rather slowly. Urban communities are typified by inner-penetration of various cultures, rapid change, and lack of agreement on values.

Many of these paired terms are overlapping. Most of them refer to folk societies in terms of intimate, face-to-face relationships, together with homogeneity of attitudes and behaviour. Urban structures, on the other hand, are characterized as being made up of more formalized and less intimate social relationships.

Solidarity in folk communities tends to be based on similarities of attitudes and behaviour, whereas solidarity in urban communities is largely a result of mutual role obligations. Relationships tend to be based on "who you are" in folk communities, but in urban communities many relationships are of a legal, contractual nature, sanctioned by a formal code of law.

Sanctions for violating social norms governing social solidarity apparently differ between these two types of communities. Durkheim's Formulation[6] states that sanctions in folk communities tend more toward repressive or punitive sanctions, but in highly developed urban societies, the sanctions are more likely to be restitutive. In the first case (repressive sanctions) the goal is likely to be punishment, but in the second case (restitutive sanctions), the motive is the maintenance of contractual obligations.

To put it another way, in folk societies,

deviant behaviour is more likely to be punished, sometimes severely. The punishment, however, is a retributive kind of punishment to make the accused suffer for his behaviour. In urban societies, according to Durkheim, there is less emphasis upon making the criminal or deviant suffer, but rather an attempt to make him pay back the "victim" for the loss. For example in urban societies when a businessman breaks a "contract," he is not made to suffer, as a rule, other than to pay the other party some money to offset the breach of contract.

We have been talking about the differences between folk social structure and roles, and urban social structure. We find, at least on the surface, a great deal of agreement among sociologists on these points of difference. What they are saying essentially is that there are vast differences on the extreme ends of the scale, between folk and urban societies. These differences can be related to our prior discussion of population and its relation to urbanization. Populations are apparently organized differently in folk societies than they are in urban societies. Not only are populations larger and more heterogeneous in urban societies, they are also organized in a more formal, less personal, and more complicated way. It is not enough to talk about the size, location, and movement of urban populations, it requires that we also talk about their patterns of human interaction in these populations. So in a sense, prior to this discussion, we have avoided one of the most important aspects of urban sociology-- the structure and function of urban populations.

We can criticize this idea of the folk-urban continuum on several counts. First, the differences between folk and urban cultures are not all that clear-cut. We might find folk cultures that are very impersonal and have an active secondary group structure. On the other hand we might find an urban culture where primary groups are very important. One further criticism of the folk-urban continuum is that it really does not tell us very much, of a very specific nature, about the differences between these two types of cultures. The continuum is expressed in very broad terms, and does not get into the complexities and subtleties of everyday life.

In advanced urban societies social structure can be looked at in several other ways. These are all social structural or functional ways of looking at the

75

city. In other words, these other approaches that we
will be discussing all try to account for how people
are "linked" together in the city, how various behaviours are coordinated, and what "function" or purpose
is being served. Again, we use <u>functional</u> in the sociological sense--meaning the relation of the parts of
society to the whole--and how the "parts" contribute to
the smooth running of the whole society.

Institutional Analysis

Institutional Analysis, for example, groups
together various parts of systems and sub-systems into
institutions. Institutions are categories that <u>cross-</u>
<u>cut empirical systems</u>, and are grouped according to
similarity of function.[7] The usual list of institutions
includes educational, legal, military, economic, religious, political, familial, and are made up of a set of
social roles and customs. The individual institution
may crosscut many organizations, associations, and groups.
For example, the family institution may include the
marriage ceremony (in a church), economic roles (in a
factory) and treatment of children in public places.
In other words, institutions are "practices" which cut
across many groups and situations.

Another way of stating what institutions
are, is to say that they are patterns of roles, quite
permanent, through which major social functions are per-
formed. Stated in this way we can see that institutions
are made up of patterns of roles. They also are quite
permanent, changing only very slowly as a rule. They
also tend to perform <u>important</u> functions. They may be
very large structures of roles, as we have mentioned,
such as "economic institution," or they may be smaller
structures of roles such as the institution of marriage.
Very large institutions such as economic institutions
may encompass thousands of organizations and groups.
Smaller institutions may involve only a few organizations and groups. The family, as an institution, for
example, involves only one group in its most limiting
sense.

A number of theorists have outlined <u>institu-</u>
<u>tional changes</u> that <u>occur as a result of urbanization</u>.
Institutions tend to change their form and function as
urbanization becomes more prevalent. These institutional changes may take hundreds of years to evolve, such
as the banking system, or they may occur more rapidly,

such as a new constitutional ammendment which changes the structure of government in a very short period of time.

The Urban Family Model[8] asserts that with increasing urbanization the family loses some of its functions and changes its internal structure as an institutional form. With the increase of educational, recreational, and social welfare organizations outside the family, many of these functions are lost. The school takes over educational functions, commercial recreation supplants family recreation, and various social welfare organizations compliment the extended family's function in providing "social security." The family is left with considerably restricted functions as a consuming unit and source of emotional support. The urban family also appears to change its structure from an extended family (three or more generations) to a nuclear family system (two generations). It has been suggested that the roles of husband and wife become more specialized, with the wife serving as a socio-emotional leader and the husband as a task leader.[9] The power alignment within the family also undergoes some changes. As the family becomes more urbanized, husband and wife are more likely to share power, making the average family more equalitarian and democratic.[10]

Radical changes in economic institutions also accompany the process of urbanization. Rapid industrialization is usually an accompaniment of urbanization. Although large cities have existed prior to industrialization, it has been only since the industrial revolution that large scale urbanization has taken place.[11] It appears that industrialization provides the necessary economic base for large concentrations of population. The rise of bureaucracy also accompanies urbanization. Again, large scale bureaucracies existed prior to the rise of large urban agglomerations, but it has been only with widespread urbanization that bureaucracy has become a world-wide dominant form of social organization. The reason for this may be that large masses of people can only be efficiently organized through bureaucratic modes of organization.

The interaction of urbanism and industrialization seem to be mutually reinforcing.[12] As urbanization increases, industrialization is more likely to take place. With increased industrialization, urbanization increases.

Stemming from this is the Service or Tertiary
Revolution which occurs with advanced stages of industrialization and urbanization. In this service revolution, increasing numbers of workers become employed in
the tertiary service sector of the economy. This trend
has progressed in the United States until now well over
half of the labor force is employed by this sector.
Just as the agricultural revolution freed workers for
employment in industry, the latter stages of the industrial revolution have freed large numbers of people for
tertiary occupations.

By tertiary occupations we mean such things
as service occupations like a barber, a stenographer,
or a lawyer. These occupations are not engaged in primary economic activities like farming or mining, nor
are they engaged in secondary economic activities like
manufacturing. Tertiary is a level above these in the
order of production, and depend, for their existance,
on the other two levels, primary and secondary. Some
have called this stage of development the Post Industrial
Society.[13]

The implications of this for the social
structures of urban areas is profound. A general upgrading of the class level has taken place, altering
the life styles of many workers and educational requirements for jobs has increased resulting in an upgrading
of the educational level. Perhaps far more important
is the fact that more jobs now require sophisticated
human relations skills, whereas in the past most workers
dealt largely with material objects.

With increased urbanism there is a rapid
growth in the size and complexity of educational institutions. Organizations concerned with education become
more elaborate, specialized, internally differentiated,
and centralized. People spend more time in school,
illiteracy is reduced and in general academic curricular
becomes more standardized and routinized. Roles become
assigned more in the society according to educational
certification than practical experience, abilities or
family status.

Perhaps we could expand this discussion
somewhat by pointing to the enormous importance of educational certification in modern societies. Schools
are the places where people are not only trained to fill
social roles later on, but schools also serve to give
diplomas, degrees, certificates and so forth.

These symbols of certification are primarily means of opening up, for the person, occupational roles that he would otherwise not have access to. We have, in urban societies, become a meritocracy, in which social roles and especially occupational roles are assigned on the basis of educational achievement. Some sociologists have gone so far as to say that the dividing line between the middle and lower classes is the college diploma. The importance of the "degree" or the diploma can hardly be over-emphasized when disucssing the social "filtering system" of modern societies. Schools and universities are the organizations that give this kind of accreditation, and only by attending (and graduating from) these places, can the average person climb the social ladder. This is often true regardless of the person's ability or intelligence.

With increasing urban growth political institutions also undergo a change. In order to coordinate the behaviour of masses of people in a complex society, the functions of government become broader and more inclusive. Political institutions tend to become more specialized and centralized with great concentrations of power occuring. These large and complex political institutions develop appended bureaucracies necessary to routinize the complex functions of the state. These trends appear to occur throughout the world in communistic, capitalistic, developed and underdeveloped countries.

Perhaps the biggest increase in complexity of governmental institutions is in the area of bureaucracy. In a country such as ours political institutions are staffed by large bureaucracies which seem to grow almost exponentially. Every new program, most changes in the law, and each new regulatory function, generates a new bureaucracy. Not only has the bureaucratic apparatus itself grown enormously in modern societies, but the number of separate autonomous (or semi-autonomous) governmental units increase to huge numbers. There are literally thousands of these separate units in the New York Metropolitan Area alone. In many cases there are overlapping jurisdictions and squabbles over jurisdiction. Just the problem of "what agency is responsible" is a constant irritant in large cities. Added to these thousands of municipal agencies and jurisdictional areas are many more thousands of State, County, and Federal agencies.

The military institutions undergo similar changes. With increasing urbanism, they become larger, and more specialized and complex.

These changes illustrate the Urbanismic-Complexity Hypothesis. This hypothesis states that as urbanism increases, there is an attendant increase in the complexity of institutions.[14]

We have tried to show in these last few pages the various ways that modern urban institutions have not only changed, but have also grown enormously in size and complexity in many cases. We showed this happening in educational institutions, in political institutions, and military institutions in particular. We have tried to show that as urbanization progresses, social organization becomes more complex, especially in its institutional forms. It would, in fact, be difficult to find an example of an institution that has become simpler and less complex as a result of urbanization. The process of complexity seems to extend to nearly every area. Not only does society become more complex with the increasing urbanization of society, but several other social structural characteristics change as well. First there appears to be an increase in the concentration of centralization of power at all levels of society.[15] This is true of organizations as well as institutions, according to Michaels.[16] It has been suggested that with the massive increase in different roles, some increase in centralization is to be expected since someone must coordinate all these roles.[17] It is unquestionably true that with urbanization there appears a proliferation of new and different roles.[18] Not only are there more roles appearing with urbanization, but there is more variety in roles, or to put it another way, more heterogeneity of roles.[19] Another social structural change we find with increasing urbanization is that institutions become more distinct from one another and more specialized in their functions.[20] Their functions become more clearly separated and each institution functions more autonomously. A number of institutional conflicts have centered around this problem of autonomy. The separation of church and state has been fought for four hundred years and is gradually being resolved by drawing a clearer line between institutional functions. The separation of civilian government and military institutions is a problem in many countries.

This separation of institutions in urban society has other secondary effects. First, there must be established some "systemic linkages" or connections

between the institutions for they cannot operate entirely apart. This requires that specialized structures be
developed to provide these connections such as the news
media which provides "feedback" from one institution to
another. Another example might be public opinion polls,
which serve the specialized function of providing general public opinion information to all or most all institutions. These linkages, in turn, often become institutionalized, such as the news media and public opinion
polls. Secondly, the functions that require the cooperation of more than one institutional structure, must be
able to call upon these various institutions at the appropriate time which requires that some cooperation between institutions be provided for.

The importance of institutional autonomy,
that develops in urban societies, lies in these difficulties outlined above including problems of integration
of institutions. In some fashion, urban societies have
to cope with the problem of institutional autonomy, and
many of the problems of such societies lies in their
inability to cope with such structures. Examples of
such difficulties might include the conflicts between
the economic sector and the government, between the
family and the schools, and between the various sub-
institutions of government itself.

Legal institutions also change as a result
of urbanization. As a society becomes more urbanized,
social order comes to depend more on formal laws and
statutes than upon informal control. The pure volume
of law increases as well as the number of areas covered
by law. This could be stated as the Urbanism-Rational-
ization Hypothesis.[21]

As urbanism increases more behaviour is
governed by universalistic law codes and organizational
rules. Maine stated this as a movement from status to
contract.[22] Durkheim expressed this change through his
discussion of Mechanical and Organic Solidarity,[23]
whereas Weber discussed it as a movement from Traditional and Charismatic Authority to Legal-Rational Authority.[24] It is important to note that the tendency toward
"rationalization" occurs in private bureaucracies as
well as public law.

By "rationalization" we mean the construction, usually quite self-consciously and purposefully
of consistent systems of rules. They are "rational" in
the same sense that they are non-contradictory. These

systems of rules also have another characteristic of rational systems, in most cases, in that they can generate, through deduction, new rules. In other words they have axiomatic-deductive characteristics. This is most easily seen in legal codes and legal procedure where the application and combination of old rules and decisions generate somewhat different, but consistent, new rules.

Although not precisely an institutional form, the associational structure of society changes when urbanization occurs. We might call this the <u>Voluntary Associations Model</u>.[25] With the growth of urbanism we find a corresponding growth in voluntary associations. Both the number of these organizations and their membership tends to grow. The reason for this also stems from the heterogeneity of the society, which generates different interest and pressure groups, who in turn organize themselves to maximize their effectiveness.[26] Kornhauser has noted that these secondary groups function as a "buffer" to insulate elites from the masses in democratic societies.[27] What Kornhauser means is that secondary groups, representing special interest groups, "filter" and channel mass or membership opinion through their leaders and the leaders in turn exert pressure on the political and economic leaders of the society. The leaders of these secondary groups, in many cases, tone down and direct into legitimate channels, in an orderly way the demands of the membership. We can see this happening in labor unions where the leaders articulate in an orderly way the sometimes confusing mixture of group opinion. At other times, they direct their membership along more moderate paths, or at least orderly procedures. As a result the economic elites in the corporation can deal with and better predict the behaviour of labor leaders and their followers. The leadership of the secondary group can, then, mute or make more predictable the behaviour of their membership.

Closely associated with the rise of voluntary associations is the <u>decline of primary groups</u>. This hypothesis expresses the idea that primary groups (e.g., the family, work, groups, et cetera), decline in importance with the rise of cities while secondary groups (e.g., unions, associations, et cetera), take on more critical functions. The secondary group presumeably assumes a greater role in socializing children and adults, are more likely to be sources of social control, and are more likely to initiate social change.[28] It has also been suggested that role models may shift from family and peers to secondary reference groups.

In our discussion of the institutional approach to urban sociology we have tried to do several things. First we have tried to show that institutional structure changes with increasing urbanization. An example of this is the growth of institutional autonomy. We have also tried to show that complexity of institutions increases as a result of urbanization. With respect to this we find many more institutional forms and sub-institutional forms, a growth in the importance of secondary groups within institutions and a decline of primary groups. Again from this perspective we find some things discovered from other approaches. We find complexity increasing with urbanization, along with an increase in the size, impersonality, and formality of the groups involved. It is probably important to take an institutional approach in urban sociology for certain theoretical problems because institutional forms are one way of seeing the organization of urban society that ties together various organizations and groups, and presents a fuller and perhaps a more dynamic picture of urban society. This approach may suffer, however, because of the ambiguity of just what constitutes an institution and the very fluidity of the concept.

Role Analysis

Our next section looks at the social structural approach from a somewhat different perspective. From the global concept of institution, we move down to the smallest element of social structure, which is the role. Here we will be examining the structure-functional approach to urban sociology from its smallest common denominator, which leads us to what we call Role Analysis, especially as it applies to urban society.

A theoretical approach implied in the structuralist perspective is Role Theory.[29] We have already shown that urban role structure differs in important ways from roles in folk societies, viewed from the perspective of the pattern variables. There are additional differences which are suggested by Simmel's Model of urban social structure.

Simmel's Theory focuses upon the dysfuncional aspects of city life, or the characteristics of urban roles which make life, less enjoyable and meaningful.[30] Although in some cases he sees social or psychological advantages to living in a city. It appears though that Simmel is talking mainly about large cities, or at least his criticisms seem to apply more to metropolitan areas than cities of 25,000 to 50,000.

Roles, he says, in urban settings tend to be heterogeneous, or there are many ways of acting and behaving. This is obviously very true and has certain important implications. It means first that people are faced with many life styles and modes of behaviour. This brings into question one's own lifestyle, beliefs, and customs, since it is obvious that there are alternative forms of belief and behaviour. There may be, therefore, a breakdown in social norms and expectations resulting in what Durkheim called anomie.[31] Anomie being a breakdown in the normative structure of the society. It should be mentioned that heterogeneity of roles implies a multitude of value orientations which are often in conflict with one another. This is exactly what happens in a large city. Varying interpretations of what is proper, or good and bad, come into conflict resulting in a number of different groups trying to discredit or destroy each other.[32] Examples of this can be seen in political party warfare, black communities allied against the police, auto workers against General Motors.

Simmel also said that urban life generates impersonality in role relationships.[33] People do not relate to each other as persons but as objects. This reminds us of Parsons' pattern variable which we related to urban structure, called affective neutrality.[34] In urban settings most relationships people encounter are impersonal or affectively neutral and not emotionally expressive. Parsons means, as does Simmel, that people play many roles in the city that express neither positive nor negative feelings. If anything, affective neutrality means an absence of emotional expression except, perhaps, a cold, impersonal, and businesslike attitude.

Impersonality implies another dimension of Parson's pattern variables, which he called Specificity. By Specificity in role relationships, Parsons means that people relate to each other in a very restricted manner. They relate as businessman to client, or as dentist to patient, not as whole persons. Their role relationships, then, in being specific, means that they are limited to specified areas of one's life and behaviour and only those areas. Urban people according to Parsons and Simmel, then, do not relate to one another as whole persons in all their variety of behaviour and attitude. Rather, they tend to find themselves forced to play rather limited role relations with many people they have to deal with. This is not to say, however, that urban people do not have some other people they can relate to as whole persons or in a broader manner, such as relatives, neighbors and friends. Simmel, in particular, seems to be saying that the urban person's role relations in public places, with bureaucracies, and in some casual encounters, have this restricted quality, but certainly not all of the urbanite's role relations are of this type.

The results of this impersonality in relationships may have wider implications for the rest of the person's life. Simmel implies that the results are often feelings of loneliness and anonymity or the feeling that one lives in a "cold" social world.[35] It further restricts the arena of self-expression to those few primary group relationships which are accessible to the person. Anonymity, as Simmel points out, may be a blessing, where one is removed from the cloying informal social controls of gossip and slander which are so typical of small towns.

Simmel also states that role relationships in urban places are often based on rational calculation, and in the extreme, dishonesty or exploitation.[36] This reminds us of Parsons' pattern variable, which he called universalism and another called self orientation.

As Parsons explains it, universalism requires that a person operate according to general (universally applied) rules.[37] Self orientation suggests that the person is more oriented toward his own interests rather than group interests.

Rational calculation implies both of these things together with perhaps a selfish and dishonest orientation toward others. Weber suggests this same urban orientation when he speaks of legal-rational authority.[38] By this he means that recently people's behaviour has come to be governed more by systemic, coldly rational rules often of a legal or quasi-legal nature, rather than by traditional customs.

If this trend is true, then some implications for urban living and personality structure must result, according to Simmel.[39] One implication is that urban people come to be distrustful and suspicious of

others. Since others are likely to be "using" you for
their own selfish ends, one must be wary. Thus barriers
are set up between people which adds even more impersonality and coldness to urban culture. A more positive
result, perhaps, according to Simmel, is that caste and
class lines tend to break down, since people are all
judged by the same, cold, hard (universalistic) rules.
One idially could be black or white, or rich or poor and
be judged on his merits. Widespread sex and race discrimination in urban societies, however, testify to the
lack of universality of standards, and a reminder that
most of us are still quite particularistic in our orientation.

One could, perhaps, criticize Simmel (and
some have) for his rather negative view of the city and
the human relationships that develop there. He may be
talking about some sections of the city, part of the
time, but to use his description of role relations as
an over-all view of city life would probably be a mistake. His emphasis upon anonymous, cold, calculating
behaviour may be more characteristic of the market-place,
or of skid-row than it is of the ordinary neighborhood.
Researchers have shown that we should make the distinction between the organized and the disorganized neighborhood. The organized neighborhood is more likely to
be socially integrated, with informal social control,
and a modicum of friendliness and comradeship. The disorganized neighborhood corresponds more to Simmel's description of the city as a place where people do not care
what happens to their neighbors and places where loneliness and anonymity is likely to exist. Simmel apparently has given us part of the picture but for the most
part, the negative view. Further along in this book we
will be looking at evidence that alienation, unfriend-
liness, and lack of human warmth are not necessarily
what we find in the city. Studies will be cited which
show high neighborliness in cities and perhaps lower
alienation than we might find in small towns. It is
very difficult to talk about the whole city and its people, especially when we are dealing with a metropolis.
It is probably more sensible to specify what part of
the city we are talking about, and what populations in
particular we are dealing with.

Almost beyond question is Simmel's conten-
tion that frequency of physical and casual social contact
is higher in urban societies.[40] A person in a large city
may rub shoulders with thousands of people during the
day, without much significant emotional expression or

meaningful relationship. The result, according to Simmel, is increased nervousness and irritability on the part of urban people. As yet this contention has not been adequately investigated or established for human populations. Among lower animals, however, high population density has profound pathological effects which has been demonstrated in a number of controlled studies. Hall,[41] however, suggests that people may be able to alter their perceptions of space and control interaction in such a way as to mitigate the effects of over-crowding.

The Japanese culture is a good example of how culture can mitigate the effects of overcrowding. Their houses and gardens are built in such a way as to create the impression of space. Culturally, the Japanese have accepted visual barriers (such as screens) as being sufficient to give one privacy, although noise may filter through these barriers. Privacy, then, comes to be defined as visual privacy. There is also some evidence that the Japanese (and other crowded people) may adapt socially to this, by creating social space which by definition is private, even though there may be many other people around. Also the Japanese and other crowded groups may learn to live with and even enjoy the presence of many people in a small space. If properly regulated, socially, many people can apparently in restricted quarters. It is perhaps the absence of effective social organization that makes crowding unbearable.

According to Simmel,[42] urban roles are also more utilitarian, thus, people in cities, he continues, are more likely to play roles for the purpose of getting a more distant goal rather than for the innate gratification of the role itself. One might, with a good deal of pulling and hauling, force this perspective into Parsons' affective neutrality dimensions, since Parsons maintains that this refers to "willingness to delay gratification."[43] However, it seems that we are talking about a good deal more than that here. We are using utilitarian not only to mean a willingness to delay gratification in urban roles, but in a general tendency to treat roles as "means" rather than "ends," and to down-grade the intrinsic importance of relationships. Some would see this not in a positive light as Parsons does, but as a dehumanization of human relationships, in general, where people become things. The opposite pole from this would be the "I-thou" relationship discussed by Buber,[44] where the relationship itself is paramount, and all instrumental or consideration of the usefulness of the relationship are secondary or even dysfunctional.

Simmel implies that the result of an instrumental role relationship is an increase in distrust and suspicion.[45] People wonder what the other person is "up to" or "what his game is."

Urban role relationships also tend to be more competitive, according to Simmel.[46] People are often trying to reach the same goal in a zero sum game situation, and one person has to lose. The upshot of this, it would seem, would be to generate even more distrust and suspicion, treating others in a utilitarian, instrumental way in an already distrustful and manipulative atmosphere. One wonders, however, to what extent this is particularly an urban phenomenon. Studies of small towns amply demonstrate the high frequency of competitive manipulation, and distrust in small-town settings. In all fairness to Simmel, however, it would seem that widespread anonymity in the cities would be condusive to the flowering of such tendencies.

Another urban tendency mentioned by Simmel which can hardly be argued with, is the development of increasingly specialized roles.[47] The sheer number of occupational categories, for example, mushrooms in an urban society. People's jobs in particular often involve very restricted role performances. The assembly line worker, of course, is a case in point. Marx, in particular, saw the roots of alienation in such a situation.[48] The worker presumedly becomes alienated not only from his work role, but from nature, family and the society in general. Marx, of course, saw the roots of modern alienation in the capitalistic system where the worker no longer had control over the means of production, and was simply an "operative" for the factory owner. Simmel has suggested here, that the roots of modern alienation lie in many more directions. He sees the city as creating a "climate" of alienation insofar as it breeds distrust, loneliness, cold economic exploitation, and superficiality. Simmel, then, goes farther than Marx and sees the whole fabric of modern urban society, not just its economic institutions, as breeding alienation of man from his society and himself.

Also, specialized roles pose some problems in terms of role conflict.[49] This conflict may stem from the fact that roles in an urban society are com-

partmentalized and are often in conflict. Thus, the
individual may be in conflict when required to fulfill
requirements of several roles at the same time or for
the same audience. Of perhaps greater importance is
the affect of this on the performer's personality organization. The person must somehow deal with the fact
that he is engaging in discontinuous and incompatible
behaviours. Unless he is able to compartmentalize or
rationalize his behaviours, intrapersonal conflict may
result. Role conflict in urban settings also occur
because of conflicting expectations for a single role.[50]
A father, for example, may be expected both to spend
time with his family and spend extra time at work.

Segmental roles that exist in the city may
have deleterious effects on community cohesion. With
a variety of specialized roles represented in a community it may become difficult to find common ground, in
the forms of value consensus, to provide a basis for
group solidarity and cohesion. This problem, of course,
reminds us of Durkheim's distinction between organic
and mechanical solidarity.[51] In urban societies the
basis of solidarity is organic, arising from interlocking roles and complementarity rather than homogeneity
of attitudes and behaviours. Solidarity within an urban
community must depend largely upon the fact that people
need each other to fill complementary roles, although
they may not necessarily agree with each other.

Durkheim's whole concept of anomie (meaning
a breakdown in social norms), is rooted in the bad effects that organic solidarity might have upon a society
and the individuals in it. In primitive societies,
anomie is not a problem, according to Durkheim, because
the basis of group solidarity is value consensus or
agreement on norms and values (which he calls, oddly
enough, mechanical solidarity). Since, by definition
such societies have agreement on norms, anomie cannot
exist, for anomie is the result of a breakdown in norms.
In modern, urban societies, however, group and societal
cohesion is no longer based upon value consensus. In
the absence of such consensus, we have by definition,
anomie, or breakdown in social norms. Here each person
is bound to the other by mutual expectations and mutual
role relationships, not like-mindedness or value consensus. Each person has his own separate job to do in
a whole chain of individual role performances. Many
people must specialize in this kind of system of inter
locking roles, in certain occupations.

89

The circle of anomie is complete when specialization itself (the roots of organic solidarity)
further divides people and breaks down commonality and
value consensus. Now many people occupy very different
positions in the social systems and as a result are
likely to develop different values.

An urban phenomenon that does not escape
Simmel's attention is the widespread use of uniforms,
badges, and other visible insignia to indicate the status
in the social structure.[52] This extends to less formal
use of language patterns, dress, and various material
accouterments to indicate social position, what kind of
person one is, and how one expects to be treated. Goffman has dealt extensively with this area in his Presentation of Self in Everyday Life.[53] These badges, signs,
and insignia serve important purposes in a large city.
They indicate to anonymous "others," who have no personal basis of judgement, how one is to be defined and
dealt with. No doubt both Simmel and Goffman are correct here, but the imputed results of this pattern are
somewhat questionable. Simmel, for example, seems to
think that such use of insignia and signs, leads to
superficiality of relationships where people come to be
judged more by status symbols than by what they really
are.[54] It might well be, however, that the very impos-
sibility of knowing anonymous others "personally" leads
to the widespread use of insignias, not vice-versa.

Simmel also points out that role relationships in large cities are likely to be transitory, a
kind of hit and run encounter, with a rapid turnover in
memberships in organizations.[55] This is presumeably a
result of the faster pace of urban society, and the
considerable horizontal and vertical mobility. The
imputed results of this transitoriness are again, more
superficiality, coldness, and segmental relationships.
In the sense that one meets more people in a large city
during a day, this hypothesis is undoubtedly true, however one might question the implications mentioned above.

Simmel also notes the importance of formal
social control in a large city, where anonymous others
must be held in check by other means than close primary
group relations.[56]

The necessity for formal controls in cities
stem from many sources, many of them poorly understood.
The most common explanation is that people in the metropolis are largely anonymous to one another and do not

know very many people in a personal way. Since informal social control requires that people know each other and respond to pressures from one another, then the possibilities for informal social control diminishes. A second explanation is the drift hypothesis, which sees the metropolis as a magnet which draws deviants to the city, who are not amenable to informal social control. A third explanation is that the very complexity of the city makes it difficult to control the population through informal means. With so many activities going on at the same time which must be articulated with one another, informal control mechanisms break down. The extensive police, quasi-police, and legal systems in cities are ample testimony to this. Little recognized, however, is the role that bureaucracies and other formalistic practices play in exercising formal social control. The assembly line, checkout counters, and closed circuit television in banks are everyday examples of non-legalistic practices which contribute to formal social control. Again we are reminded how close this formulation fits Weber's contention that legal-rational forms of authority are becoming predominant in modern urban society.[57] Formal social control can be seen as a substitute for informal social control that exists in smaller folk societies where every person controls the other in his day-to-day personal interaction.

In this section, dealing with role analysis with respect to the city, we have focused upon the work of Georg Simmel. He has mentioned many urban role characteristics which mesh quite well with the pattern variables of Parsons' discussed earlier. Among other things Simmel makes reference to the impersonality, manipulativeness, suspicion, anonymity and loneliness of role relations in the city. We have criticized his position, previously, by pointing out that his analysis is quite negative and that he sees human relationships in the city to a great extent as being destructive of human happiness. We have pointed out that there is a more positive side to urban role relationships, and that it is very difficult to make blanket statements about urban people and their relationships in general, when it is quite obvious that there are many different kinds of neighborhoods and other areas within the city which have different role relationships and cultures. We have further suggested that it might make more sense to look at each area of the city separately, or at least, group them according to type, before making any general statements. We may, in other words, have to look at the city in parts before we can make statements

91

about the whole.

Role analysis, however, is an important
part of analyzing the social structure of the city,
since roles are the basic units of any social system.
Other ways we have looked at the city, such as institutional analysis, depend upon some understanding of urban
role relationships. Also role analysis fills out our
understanding of the social structure of the city, in
and of itself.

At this point we would like to shift to
some slightly different kinds of structures that have
not been dealt with before in this text, but are important elements of urban life. We are talking here mainly about power structures and status systems, which
pervade not only the local community but the whole society. We think it is important to deal with these
structures because they have such an impact upon other
aspects of urban life, and because they tend to reflect
underlying organization of people in all societies, not
just urban ones.

Power Structure

There is some controversy over what we mean
by power structure or for that matter what we mean by
the term power. Some see power as a potential to alter
other's behaviour by force, but only a potential which
need not be activated to be real. Others see power as
the actual imposition of force on others to cause them
to change their behaviours, and not just a potential.
Still others would not restrict the word power to the
use of force. They would include suggestion, imitation,
and expectation. They would say that whenever one person (or group) can cause a change in behaviour in another person, they have power over that person. It is
precisely around these different definitions that contradictory findings in the studies of power and power
structures arise. If we could agree on what power is,
then perhaps there could be some agreement on the findings of empirical studies.

The meaning of Power Structure is also subject to great controversy and as a result makes interpretations of community power studies difficult. Some
see power structures,again, as potential wielders of
power, who need not actually wield the power. Others
maintain that power structures, to be designated as such,

must show evidence of the use of power. As if this did
not cause enough difficulty in the study of community
power structure, there are still other differences between researchers in how they conceptualize power structures and therefore how they measure them or assess them.
Some researchers begin their studies with the assumption
that there is a small group of "leaders" at the top of
every community that pretty much decide the important
decisions, and as a result set out to find out who these
leaders are, and perhaps how their leadership filters
down to lower levels of decision makers.[58] They have,
what has been called, an elitist view of community power structure. Because they begin with an elitist model
they often find it because their research methods look
for and find people at the top. Other researchers begin
their studies with the view that many different groups
hold power in the community and design their research
accordingly. They go about looking for different power
groups and identifying them. Again, their methods often
produce the results they expect. They often find a
pluralistic structure of power, that is, power exercized
by many groups not just one group at the top.[59] A third
group of researchers start with the assumption that
there is no single power structure, but rather two or
more competing groups who are engaged in conflict with
one another. They, then, set about looking for conflicting power groups and often find them, partly because of
the way they have set about examining the problem. They
see community power as conflict.[60]

          In those cases where researchers have used
more than one method of discovering the power structure
of a community, there is often conflicting results.
Some communities seem to be best described as a single
power elite, others are better described as a number of
separate power groups, and sometimes the conflict model
seems more appropriate.[61]

          At the present time it appears that differ-
ent communities have different kinds of power structures.
It also appears that how one studies power structure
has a great impact on the kind of power structure one
uncovers in a city.

Status Systems

          People in all societies are also organized
on a status hierarchy according to the "esteem" they
are granted by others. This in turn seems to be a re-

sult of the style of life a person engages in.[62]

By style of life we mean how a person spends his money, his time, and his energy. It also involves the hobbies he engages in, his interests of an avocational nature and the kind of people he associates with. One person might spend all his extra time and money at the race track, others watching television, and still others going to plays, concerts, and operas.

Status placement in urban societies is problematical in many respects. First, there are so many different life styles, it becomes difficult to evaluate and rank them. The average person cannot rank on one dimension all the varied life styles of a community. Secondly, there is the problem of individuals having more than one status in urban societies. In folk societies statuses are almost always congruent with respect to a single individual or groups of individuals.[63] In urban societies people often occupy a number of different status positions with different expectations and levels of esteem attached to them. This results in what has been called <u>status inconsistency</u>.[64] The classic example is the Black physician.

The Black physician has a low status as a result of being Black, but a high status as a result of being a physician. The result is confusion in his own mind, (and in other's minds) where to place him on the status ladder, and how to treat him as a person. Other classic examples of status inconsistency is the poorly educated truck driver who earns $25,000 a year, or the self-made man who came from a poor background but has come to be a rich businessman. The list is very long of examples of status inconsistency among members of our society and to some degree, probably includes most of us. The basic importance of the concept of status inconsistency is that it makes it difficult for the person to evaluate his own worth and for others to judge him. This, in some cases, may create personality disturbances in the individual.

It may be that status inconsistency is rather common in urban societies. Women, in a business or professional role, encounter this difficulty, as do members of minority groups. It appears that urban societies generate more role differentiation, which in turn increases the probability of status inconsistency. We might call this the <u>Urbanization-Status Inconsistency Hypothesis</u>.

94

Social Class

A final structural dimension of urban society is Social Class. In folk societies, class divisions either do not exist at all, or emerge in clear-cut readily-apparent form. The class structure of Medieval Europe was of this nature. Serfs were clearly marked off from the nobility, which in turn were clearly separated from the clergy.[65] A small middle class composed of traders, artisans and others was just beginning to develop. In urban societies class divisions are much less clear-cut, as the variety of conflicting typologies of social class indicate.[66]

The numbers of different classes enumerated by sociologists, alone, range from three to over ten. Some use the term "working class" as a euphemism for lower class, others do not use the term at all. Some have used the reputational approach, asking people to place others in a social class, which produces a class structure different from other approaches. Other researchers have used the subjective approach, asking the person to rate his own social class position.[67] This also produces a different structure. Still others use an "objective" approach, using the sociologist's own criteria of what constitutes a person's class position such as wealth or education. There is, therefore, very little agreement beyond the fact that people do vary in their own subjective view of their class, and that sociologists can rank, in some sort of manner, the class positions of individuals. Despite this apparent confusion, social class is a very important variable in the study of communities, since it tends to be related to a host of sociological variables. It is so important, in fact, that no competent researcher would conduct a survey without some measure of social class as a way of classifying people. It is also apparent that the social class structure of a city is an important way of organizing people and it must be understood before much headway can be made in understanding a city. It is related to politics, population movement, and a host of urban dynamics.

General Theories of Stratification and Urbanization

There are a number of general theories of stratification which suggest some relationships with urbanizations. The most popular in American sociology is Weber's division of stratification into class, status and power,[68] which we have used as the basis of our previous discussion. Here, each stratification dimension is assumed to have a somewhat different basis. Status is based upon the prestige accorded various styles of life. Groups of people with a similar style of life are called status groups by Weber, which in their extreme form become endogamous castes.

Power, according to Weber,[69] is based upon the ability to modify the behaviour of others and is acquired somewhat independently from status or class.

Class position, according to Weber, is based upon one's "life chances," which is directly related to one's economic position in society.

Weber's conception of stratification has been widely labeled the multidimensional approach, and has the advantage of conceptual clarity.[70] Weber, in other words, saw social stratification as a complex phenomenon, involving at least three dimensions namely, class, status, and power. He saw a degree of correlation between these three dimensions, but in many cases they did not fit exactly. For example, there is a tendency for persons with a given status position to occupy similar class positions. Likewise, persons with high power are likely to have high status and class positions. Weber saw, however, that there were enough exceptions to these parallelisms, to treat class, status and power as separate dimensions. The relevance of all of this to urban sociology is to point out that there are many systems or dimensions of social stratification not just one. To look at the city as just a three-class system based on wealth, would over-simplify the problem. Weber gives us a number of ways of approaching urban stratification systems not just one. With his conceptualization, we may look separately at the power structure, the status (or life style) patterns, and the class structure. American sociologists, however, have tended in their empirical work on cities, to lump together a number of separate variables including life style, economic position, and education and call it social class. This has added more confusion to the whole problem of social stratification and the study of it in cities.

It appears, that with greater urbanization these clear-cut systems of class, status, and power may break down and Weber's model may be a much too simple representation of the facts. In highly urbanized societies there may be a variety of competing status groups, each based on a somewhat different style of life. Likewise, rather than one hierarchy of power, there is often a number of hierarchies in a pluralistic society. Even the concept of class gets somewhat confused under these circumstances. With increasing urbanization there may be a fragmentation of stratification hierarchies in which these systems become much more complex and differentiated.

Weber's stratification theory, it should be pointed out, was an answer to Karl Marx, who had earlier asserted that social class alone was sufficient to describe the stratification system of a society.[71] Marx saw each social class in all societies as having similar life styles, economic position, and power. According to Marx (and this is treated in an expanded manner in other sections of the book), there is an elite strata in every society, or at least above the level of primitive communisms. This strata controls the life styles, status positions, and life chances of all the other strata. It does this because it controls the means of production, or the productive capacity of the society.[72] Even religion, education, and the arts express the "class interests" of the ruling elite strata. They are, in every sense of the word, dominant. He was especially interested in capitalistic societies at various stages of urbanization, and saw the rising "working class" as the new elite who would challenge and eventually overcome the elite (the capitalists). The new society would be a "worker-controlled" society. It is easy to see that Marx saw social class in urbanizing societies as a conflict situation, with class pitted against class. Many contemporary sociologists, especially in Europe, analyze the contemporary urban malaise from this Marxian perspective.

The application of this theory to urban sociology is quite straight-forward. As urbanization and industrialization progresses, the control over the means of production changes hands from one elite group to another. For example, at the end of the feudal period in Europe, power passed from the landed aristrocacy to the bourgeoisie. When workers wrest control over the means of production from the bourgeoisie, according to Marx,[73] power will presumeably be vested in the hands of the workers. This process will involve the development of class conciousness and ensuing class struggle. In short, Marxist theory asserts that the class (power and status) structure is a function of who controls the means of

97

production. As the means of production (technology) changes the class structure must change.[74] And urbanization and technological progress inevitably produces changes in the means of production. Marx did not, however, mean that "economic" factors were the only determinants of class structure. He has asserted that they were the most important ones. Finally, at the end of the historical process, when urbanization and technology become highly developed, a classless society presumably emerges.[75]

The Functional Theory of stratification in relation to urbanization.[76] suggests another way to view the stratification process. This theory states that the amount of prestige and rewards a given occupation offers is a function of how important that position is to the social system. Garbage collecting is a relatively unimportant function in the society. Physicians, on the other hand, have high prestige and remuneration because human health is a basic and important prerequisite to societal well being.

Functional Stratification Theory is not quite that simple, however, and few if any would agree with such a simple formulation of the problem. The functionalists also go on to enumerate other factors that might account for differences in prestige and monetary rewards among occupations. One other factor they suggest is the degree of training required for the performance of an occupation. An occupation that requires very little training would tend to (but not always) offer very limited rewards and prestige. An exception to this in a city like New York City might be the garbage collector who can gross $15,000 a year with a minimum of education, or the Ph. D. who is driving a cab for much less money. The functionalist view of stratification also sees "scarcity of talent" as a factor determining differential prestige. A relatively unimportant job may attract few men who want or are able to perform it. An example of this migh be the rare individual who has an unusual capacity for "wine-tasting." Finally, the functionalists see the "unpleasantness of the task" as a factor in giving an occupation a particularly high reward structure. Examples of this might be the garbage collector, the pearl diver, or the underwater demolition expert.

The relationship of this to urbanization has not been explored but it would appear that as urbanization increases the importance and nature of various occupations change.[77] Thus we find that as urbanization increases, specialized occupations become more crucial, occupations requiring more training expand, and occupations involving the manipulation of people rather than "things" take on a new importance. To this degree we would expect that such occupations would increase in prestige and as a result the class structure would change. Parsons has stated that the distribution of social rank depends on the functional problems facing the society at any given time.[78]

We have already shown, however, in our discussion of functionalist stratification theory, that such a limited view of social ranking is inadequate. We have shown many exceptions to the "simple" functional view that people are stratified according to the importance of their function. There may, however, be a great deal of truth to Parsons' assertion, given these many exceptions.

It is also apparent that as societies become more urbanized, occupations are assigned more on the basis of competence than on ascription as in the past. Thus, possibly, the functional stratification theory applies more to urbanized societies than it does to pre-urban societies.

Related to this functional theory is the Laissez Faire Capitalistic Theory of Supply and Demand which simply states that the price of labor is a function of the supply of labor and the demand for labor in any given occupational group.[79] If the supply of physicians, for example, is low and the demand (functional importance) is high the wages obtained by physicians will be high (at the point of the intersection of supply and demand curves). This result occurs only under perfect conditions of a free market. Unfortunately, these conditions seldom apply. Collusion and manipulation of the market occurs as well as imperfect knowledge of the market. Nepotism, favoritism, and seniority all serve to base the cost of labor, to some extent, on "ascriptive" criteria. Ascription, then, is still a significant force in determining status systems in urban societies.

We have examined several different ways of conceptualizing status systems and power structures. We have found that there is little agreement as to the class structures and power structures of urban societies. We have found varying views ranging from conflict theory which emphasizes the warring factions of society to views of status systems as merely different styles of life,

such as the differences between the way a day laborer
lives and the way a Wall Street lawyer lives. There
does seem to be some agreement that strata exist in
urban societies, whether they be power groups, status
groups, or class levels. The difficulty occurs when
sociologists and political scientists attempt to assess
the precise form and dynamics of these strata. It is
obvious, though, that power structures and status systems (or class systems) are important organizing elements in urban societies and much work needs to be done
to clarify them, and that stratification is an important
part of urban social organization.

We have talked about different ways of looking at the social structure of the city, as social systems, institutional forms, role structures, and power
and status (or class) systems. Each approach has its
advantages and disadvantages depending upon the kind of
problem to be examined, and the theoretical orientation
of the investigator. In this next section we would like
to deal with a structural approach, called the Mass
Society model, which attempts to conceptualize entire
urbanized societies. In various ways these urban societies can be described in terms that apply to all cities
within an urbanized society, and be made to characterize the important dynamics and characteristics of such
a society. This next section, then, will be a highly
macroscopic and broad approach, which perhaps can be
useful in gaining a fuller view of the entire urban society.

Mass Society Theory

We have noted that urban areas (e.g., cities,
metropolitan areas, megalopolii) are easily upset by
forces extrinsic to them. This problem of macro systemic influence can best be summerized by discussing
Mass Society Theory.[80] Although there is lack of clarity
in most discussions of what a mass society model entails,
it is clearly a phenomena which develops along with increasing urbanization. In particular, it refers to broad
social-psychological and structural characteristics which
pervade highly urbanized societies. These generate forces which are usually national in scope, and are often
organized on a national basis. These societal urban
forces can be subsummed under two broad headings of
structural and social-psychological.

Mass society theory seems to center around

several facts about contemporary urban society. First, cities and smaller centers are subject to powerful societal forces external to the local areas. These forces are usually mass phenomena involving large numbers of people. These structural, mass, forces have a social-psychological impact on individuals in the society.[81]

One major structural variable involved in mass society theory is that of mass communcation. By mass communication we mean one-way communication between media and the mass where many people receive identical massages from the media without the opportunity of significant feedback.[82] Examples of such systems are the publishing industry, television, radio and the design of products. Mass communication (e.g., the mass media) are interrelated to all other dimensions of mass society, just as all dimensions of mass society are related and are mutually interdependent with each other. The mass media is especially crucial to the whole system of modern (e.g., urban) societies. In fact, we might say that the mass media is the primary source of moral integration in modern societies. It is from the mass media that public opinion becomes crystalized, organized, reinforced and disseminated. It is the mass media that lends an air of authority to amorphous and developing mass opinion. The mass media not only organizes and disseminates public opinion, it molds and creates it in urban societies. This is not to say that the mass media creates all or most opinions in such societies but rather it serves to reinforce some opinions and ignores others.

Its role becomes more clear in its relation to economic institutions. One of its functions is to create mass demand for goods and services of subscribers. It does this primarily through advertising. It creates through this medium not only mass demand but uniform mass demand. It is not enough to create demand alone, for industry requires a uniformity of demand so that goods can be mass-produced.[83] Mass production is the primary mode of achieving economies of scale in such societies. Thus public opinion must be molded by the mass media to demand similar kinds of goods. This is true even though businessmen attempt to differentiate their products from those of their competitors.

The mass media also serves mass politics in a similar manner. Support is generated for candidates, parties, and policies through the mass media. In societies with large and heterogeneous populations, this is

101

the only practical way to organize political action.
The potential of mass politics becoming irrational and
manipulative has been discussed widely.[84] One outcome
is the manipulation of the media by powerful interest
groups to alert public opinion. An alternative model
of mass communication suggests that this kind of manipulation is reduced by a two-step flow of communication.[85]
This model suggests that mass communications are filtered
by the primary group structure before they reach the
individual. Usually a "gate-keeper" in each group eval-
uates and transmits selected information, thus the individual is shielded from the full impact of the media.
If the media transmits messages contrary to group standards, they will be rejected. It may also be the case
that secondary groups provide similar "filtering" functions, through official statements, policies, and news-
letters. In any case it appears that an atomistic model
of media impact must be ammended to include such considerations. It seems reasonable that some such mechanisms
would have to be developed to enable the individual to
deal with the increase in information that accompanies
urbanization.

Another structural characteristic of "mass
society" appears to be mass organization.[86] The more
urbanized a society the larger and more powerful organizations become, which are organized on a mass basis
and are national in scope and influence. They are often
extremely powerful and exert influence far beyond their
numbers. The individual faced with mass organization
often feels powerless and ineffective.

Examples of mass organizations are numerous
in an urbanized society. We might start with the example of powerful corporations in our society which control
a large proportion of our productive capacity. These extremely large corporations are now in the process of
becoming multinational corporations with power and influence throughout the world. The worker faced with
such great power cannot help feeling a little overwhelmed. A second type of mass organization designed
to counterbalance the large corporate organizations are
the large labour unions, who claim approximately
20,000,000 members in this country alone. These unions
are also powerful organizations, over which the individual worker has little or no control. It has also been
suggested that, in many cases, the large unions work in
collusion with corporation in controlling both the workers and price of products. Although there are many
other examples of large mass organizations such as uni-

versity systems, foundations, religious bodies, and political parties, perhaps the largest mass organization and the possibly most powerful, is the Federal government which has access to the basic instruments of military power, legislative power and executive power. A brief look at the enormous Federal government budget (about 900 billion per year) is an indication of the enormous power involved. Added to this level of government, of course, is the collective power of State, County, and Local governments. It is little wonder that the average citizen, in an urbanized country, feels overwhelmed by the power of large organizations.

Mass movements are another structural feature of urbanized, mass societies. They represent in rudimentary form, the organization of masses of people ignored by established elites.[87] They may be considered, for some purposes, counter-elites. They are often made up, initially, of dis-affected, alienated individuals, many of whom do not fit into conventional roles. Mass movements are vehicles of significant social change in highly urbanized societies, and although they rarely accomplish all of their goals, often change the society to some extent. Their major function may be to provide an outlet for frustration and alienation generated by the established structures.

During the 1960's we saw a flood of such mass movements which mobilized the energies of millions of people. Although the Anti-War Movement was the most dramatic of these movements there were many others, some related and others not related to the war in Viet Nam. All of these movements served as outlets for frustrations generated in a changing urban society. The Civil Rights Movement was certainly a protest movement which had its roots in hundreds of years of prejudice and discrimination. It mobilized the energies of Whites as well as Blacks, and Southerners as well as Northerners. Like most movements of this kind it was composed of many different factions and a variety of approaches. The Civil Rights Movement had a characteristic which served as a model for many of the other movements of the period. This characteristic was the demand for human rights and the right for justice and equal treatment. Other movements of the time shared this perspective including the Feminist Movement, the Gay Movement, and the Mental Patients' Movement. Other movements of the period having somewhat the same human rights perspective were the Drug Movement and the so-called Hippie Movement. The mass nature of these movements could be seen in the scope of their operations, their national character, and the large number of adherents.

Mass entertainment is a highly significant structure in mass society, for several reasons. Mass entertainment presents "impersonal" role-models to millions of people which often conflict with community values and may undermine these values.[88] Now millions of people may identify with heroes they have never met, or know very little about. As a result "personal identity" in a mass society can be based on limited personal experience. The implications of this for personality development in urban society has yet to be fully explored. It may, however, result in superficiality of urban personality mentioned by some urbanologists.

Not only do urban heroes have an impersonal quality but they are also constantly changing. Yesterday's hero may be the fool of today. The charming "Gidget" of the 50's is replaced by the hippie freak of the 60's. Conflicting role models are constantly being perfected in the mass media, also. The result may be the creation of fluid and conflicting identities. This has yet to be explored.

The consequences of mass society structures have already been hinted at. Aside from the fact that mass society structures influence community values, it is clear that local communities are greatly affected in other ways by these structures.[89] Many of the organizations in communities are based outside of the community, and are mass organizations.

Theoretically, a number of psychological changes in individuals should flow from the nature of mass society.[90] It has been suggested by Karl Marx and others that mass production creates in the worker's mind a feeling that he is expendible and not very important. The work that he is engaged in is tedious and repetitive diminishing his growth as a person. He is also likely to feel powerless and experience a feeling of meaninglessness due to his subservient and demeaning role. Marx has even suggested that this alienation from work can carry over into other areas of the worker's life, estranging him from himself, family, society, and God. Mass communication may well result in meaninglessness also as the individual is flooded with a variety of meaning systems, often having little relevance to his everyday life. He may also have a sense of being manipulated by the mass media as he is innundated by a flood of propaganda and advertising. Mass organization in the form of large scale organization may confront the person with monolithic group pressure and power giving him a feeling of powerlessness. Mass entertainment may reduce the person to a spectator again making him feel ineffectual. Mass entertainment also may confuse the person with a parade of distant and impressive identity models. On the positive side mass entertainment may lighten the drudgery of everyday work. Mass movements may also have a positive effect in providing the person with an outlet for feelings of powerlessness and meaninglessness to the extent that he becomes involved in them. To the extent that these movements add to the confusion of everyday life, they may create an even greater feeling of meaninglessness and powerlessness. Mass politics may confront modern man with a sense of powerlessness and being manipulated. He may, as a result, feel even more suspicious and isolated.

In our discussion of mass society theory we have dwelt mainly on the negative aspects of such an urban society. At this point it is appropriate to point out some positive outcomes of such a mass society. First of all, mass movements, as we have pointed out, provide a release for pent up frustration and give citizens a way of making changes in their society. Mass organization, for all its potential for alienation of workers, does seem to be the most efficient form of organizing the energies of millions of people in a complex society. It provides a structure for action that might otherwise result in chaos, or a breakdown in the society. For example, large-scale government seem to be the only efficient way to govern hundreds of millions of people. Large corporations enable the society to concentrate the enormous amounts of capital and trained manpower necessary for large economic undertakings. Large unions enable the relatively helpless single worker to join with others in protecting his economic rights and economic progress. In sum, large complex urban societies, to some degree require large scale organizations and movements to keep the society integrated and functioning.

Mass society theory, in summary, attempts to give a societal-wide view of urban societies, focusing especially upon their _mass_ characteristics. We have enumerated to a degree the ways in which this _mass_ society can be described by referring to mass organization, mass movements and so forth. Mass society theory is not in conflict with any of the other perspectives we have discussed in this book. In fact, mass society theory compliments and adds to the more limited population, ecological, and other social organizational theories.

It focuses upon the large-scale organizations and movements in our urban society in a way that the other theories previously discussed have not.

In a negative vein, mass society theory at this point is extremely sketchy in its outline of urban societies. It gives the main outlines of such societies but leaves out the precise way in which these large organizations and movements operate and contribute to the functioning of the whole. In other words this theory is extremely general and needs to be more fully completed. Secondly, this theory may over-emphasize the importance of large-scale and societal-wide organization in urban societies. These societies, are after all, composed of a variety of small groups, associations, and informal neighborhood and community relations.

Functionalism

Our final section dealing with structural-functional theories of cities, deals explicitly with functionalism as an approach to understanding social organization. We have already discussed previously, the basic meaning of functionalism in sociology and the kind of perspective it takes. At this point all we wish to do is to recapitulate some of the points already made about functionalism and to expand this discussion to some degree. It is important to realize, however, that we have dealt with and discussed functionalism to a considerable degree prior to this chapter and that much of it will not be repeated.

Part of our reasons for making a special section dealing with functionalism is to introduce the idea of the functional prerequisites of societies and cities, and finally to expound various theories of dysfunctions or non-functional aspects of cities.

Functionalism had its roots in the work of Durkheim,[91] Malinowski and Radcliffe-Brown.[92] Their approach was to view societies as systems, and various practices, beliefs and behavior patterns as having a function in maintaining those systems. Functional, meant a contribution to the smooth running of the social system. Basically the question posed was, how does this practice or belief fit into the whole system and contribute to the functioning of the society? Some awareness has recently developed regarding the inadequacy of a functionalism that just deals with system functions. A case in point is Wrong's and Etzioni's work. Wrong has conceptualized the problem in terms of sociology's "over-socialized view of man," which assumes people can and do adapt to any social system requirement.[93]

What he means by this is that sociologists have been too prone to assume that people can and do adapt to any kind of social requirement or society. Sociology has failed to see that "human nature" has limits of endurance and that society (despite its social system requirements) must stay within these limits. He implies that sociologists have neglected the "needs" of the average man in focusing too much on the needs of the social system.

Etzioni has phrased his criticism by sug-gesting that individual needs must be taken into account in any theory of social behaviour.[94] Again, Etzioni is suggesting that human beings have "needs" (a taboo word in sociology) and that these needs must be taken into account in analyzing and constructing social systems. People, then are not just blank pieces of paper to be written on by society, but have biologically rooted and socially patterned needs that every "good" society should attempt to satisfy.

These criticisms suggest that the function-ality of a society as a smoothly-running system in equi-librium is not the only kind of functionality that should be considered in analyzing a society. A society, such as Nazi Germany, may have been smoothly functioning as a system but in the process of its development, killed six million Jews and untold others who they felt were their enemies. A corporation in the United States may be a smoothly run operation but turn out useless or even harmful products. The Segregationist South was a smooth-ly running system in equilibrium but held in abject bondage for many years many millions of Black people, causing untold deaths and abject suffering. So a social system may be functional as a system in smoothly-running equilibrium, but be very non-functional (or dysfunction-al) for many people living in it, and neglect very basic human needs.

With these reservations in mind, we may proceed to analyze the relevance of functional theory for urban sociology. Several sociologists have attempted

to outline the functional problems faced by societies
in general, including urban societies.

Parsons, for example, has set forth four
main functional problems faced by any society. He includes the functions of adaptation, goal attainment,
pattern maintenance, and integration.[95] Adaptation
refers to the necessity of society adjusting to its
environment and becomes a specialty of the economic institutions. Goal attainment refers to the task of a-
chieving definite goals of the society and the individual, which becomes a specialty of political institutions.
Pattern maintenance refers to the task of maintaining
the cultural integrity of the society, by regulating
norms, values, and symbolic systems. This becomes a
specialty of religious and educational institutions.
Integration is a function which deals with the integration of roles in society, and is a specialty of the societal community.

Parsons can be criticized here mainly by
the superficiality and generality of his list of functional problems that have to be solved by any society
or any city. The list could probably be expanded (and
simplified) considerably to carefully outline the thousands of functions a city as a system or series of systems has to contend with. Again, more urbanized communities tend to separate these functions far more than
folk communities.[96] Loomis has extended the list to
include communication, boundary maintenance, systemic
linkage, and institutionalization.[97] Here too, these
functions are more separated in urban communities.

We have already pointed out that institutions in urban communities are more autonomous and that
they, themselves, are further sub-divided into more specialized functions. In tribal societies (or pre-literate societies) there is little specialization either in
roles or institutions, whereas in urbanized societies,
we find a great deal of specialization, and functional
differentiation.

We see in these functional problems further
examples of the Urbanization-Functional Differentiation
Hypothesis which states in its most general form that
the more urbanized a community or society, the greater
is the differentiation of function that takes place.[98]

The list of functional requirements of urban
areas could probably be extended much further to include

108

the functions of higher education, recreation, mass movements, et cetera, in maintaining an urban social system. Much of our previous discussion implies a number of functional relationships in other contexts.

It has been noted that deviant or even illegal activities may be functional to the maintenance of an urban social system. Whether this is particularly characteristic of urban societies is open to question. The Cosa Nostra, for example, provides services for the public which are unavailable through legitimate means. Merton has noted that the political boss system provided services to the public which were greatly needed, even though machine politics engage in illegal or questionable practices.[99]

There are a number of other functional differences and characteristics we find especially in urban societies, which we will now discuss.

Another aspect of functional analysis which Merton has noted is the differentiation between latent and manifest functions.[100] Latent functions are the unanticipated or unplanned for results of a given practice. Manifest functions are expected and recognized results of a given social practice. The latter are a result of rational planning and foresight, the former are not. This has important consequences for all societies. Often latent functions provide the basis for new social institutions, or in other cases they cause greater problems. Urban societies, being more rationalized, are based more upon manifest functions. Folk societies, however, which invoke less rational design of social systems are characterized more by latent functions. Another way to state this is to say that modern urban societies are constructed more by rational calculation which attempts to assess beforehand, any consequences of a given practice. Just the fact that urban societies are more analytical about their social systems, means that there will be more conscious awareness of functional relationships. In other words people in urban societies will understand more so than their preliterate or folk culture counterparts, the reasons for various social practices, the way these practices fit in with each other, and the practical consequences of such practices. Some people, probably middle and upper status people, will be more aware of these functional relationships than others. Nevertheless, in urban societies and cities there will be, in general, greater awareness of the various functions that each part plays in the society and to some extent their problematical nature, or possibility for improvement.

The Folk-Urban Continuum points to these differences in orientation. Not only are urban societies more likely to use rational calculation, they are less likely to be tradition oriented and less likely to question the basis of any given part of the culture.[101] At the folk end of the continuum there is less likelihood that there will be social change and innovation, thus less likelihood of rational planning. Traditional oriented societies by definition are based upon relatively unquestioned acceptance of what is regardless of the consequences. Another way to state this is to say that in folk societies all functions tend to be latent in the sense that functional relationships are not generally recognized. This is not to say, however, that people in folk societies do not individually calculate the effects of their behaviour in terms of their own self interests. It is clear that they do. What is lacking is any widespread recognition of the part that individual and social practices play in maintaining the social system as a whole.

As urbanization progresses, legal and moral codes as well as a proto-science develop which increasingly recognizes functional relations in society.[102] Hammurabe's code, the old testament, and the writings of the Greeks are examples of this. In our time the quest to change latent into manifest is a preoccupation of both the sciences and technology. In short, rationality and prediction are hallmarks of urban civilization.

Dysfunctions

Functional theory also calls attention to dysfunctions within societies. Dysfunctions are practices which disrupt the smooth functioning of a social system and throw it out of equilibrium. As we have said social practices can also be dysfunctional for the satisfaction of human needs of individuals in the society.[103] The implication that "dysfunctional" always means "undesireable" has been discussed elsewhere and is certainly to be avoided.[104]

With this reservation in mind, let us proceed with the consideration of dysfunction in urban societies and related hypotheses.

A global hypothesis which is _implied_ in much sociological theory is the Hypothesis of Urban Depravity. This hypothesis in its most general form states that the city life is degrading and dehumanizing, and that the moral basis of society is rural.[105] In its more scholarly and sophisticated form cities' increasing alienation, depersonalization, and neurosis as society grows more urban. Sophisticated social scientists often mute their criticisms by referring to advantages of urban life or by taking a neutral stance toward their findings.[106]

Some of the most influential behavioural scientists have taken such a position and in effect supported the "urban depravity" hypothesis. Simmel is perhaps the most widely known critic of the cities in citing the negative outcomes of crowding, nervous innervation, competitiveness, dishonesty, loneliness, and superficiality.[107] Other well-known figures have also contributed their reservations concerning the adverse effects of urban life. Freud, for example, clearly viewed urbanization with a jaundiced eye. In Civilization and Its Discontents he concludes that urbanism involves increasing suppression of libidinal energy, redirecting it into acceptable channels, and through such massive sublimation, creating neurosis. Eventually, he concludes, all civilization will crumble.[108]

Marx also saw increasing urbanization as resulting in ever increasing degrees of dehumanization and alienation of the average man. The only (inevitable) solution, he concludes, is the development of a communistic society in which an orderly anarchism will prevail.[109] At this time urbanism and industrialism will culminate in a "perfect" society in which all men can actualize themselves.

Max Weber, although not strongly anti-urban, pointed out the dangers of a world increasingly dominated by legal-rational authority especially in the form of modern bureaucratic systems.[110] The danger, he asserted, is the dehumanization of people who are increasingly treated as impersonal objects in bureaucratic settings. Emile Durkheim also saw dangers inherent in the social organization that holds modern urban societies together.[111] He asserted that anomie or normlessness is characteristic of heterogeneous, mobile societies where norms are unstable and changing.

This hypothesis has not yet been adequately tested. Nevertheless, it has had an important

111

influence on the way that urbanism has been viewed.

A related hypothesis is the Urban Decline Hypothesis. In a general way it states that urban societies and especially large cities become increasingly unliveable as urbanization increases.[112] Again, this hypothesis has not been adequately tested, partly due to the lack of agreement among sociologists regarding the nature of personality system requirements. Given this fact, it is virtually impossible to make statements about the quality of urban life beyond some criteria of biological survival. Nevertheless, social scientists and laymen alike have mentioned that the quality of urban life is declining.

Philip Hauser, in his American Sociological Association Presidential Address, The Chaotic Society: Production of the Social Morphological Revolution, strongly endorses this hypothesis.[113] Not only does he feel that urban life is declining but that it will get worse as time passes. He mentions the problem of housing, transportation, pollution, racial conflict, delinquency, crime, drug addiction and mental disorder, among others. These problems he maintains, are direct results of the transition from a folk society to an urbanized society with its attendant shift in institution forms. Perhaps some light can be shed on this hypothesis by examining derivative sub-hypotheses which postulate dysfunctional outcomes in urban society.

The first sub-hypothesis is the Urbanization-crime Hypothesis. This hypothesis asserts that as urbanization increases, crime increases.[114] The difficulty in testing such a hypothesis is the absence of national crime statistics prior to 1933 in the United States. A second problem is unrealiability of crime statistics which can be affected by reporting variations. There are many other sources of error but "reporting" is probably the main one.[115]

Since 1933 there has been a marked increase in the crime rate which of course, supports the hypothesis.[116] Also more urbanized areas tend to have higher crime rates than less urbanized areas, which again lends support to the hypothesis.[117] On the other hand, there are indications that crime rates were as high or even higher prior to 1933, although the evidence is confined to single cities, or unsystematic evidence.[118] It appears that in the short run, at least, the hypothesis is supported, but there is some doubt about long-term trends.

A closely related hypothesis is the Urbani-
zation-Civil Disorder Hypothesis. This hypothesis holds
that with increasing urbanization, civil disorder also
increases.[119] Rather than cite individual studies the
reader is referred to the report of the President's
Commission on Violence which had reviewed much of the
relevant information.[120] Their review of cross-nation-
al studies shows that civil disorder and violence are
more prevalent among countries with a low degree of urbanization.

A hypothesis that has recently gained favor
is the Urbanization-Ecological Crisis Hypothesis.[121]
This hypothesis states that as urbanization increases,
there is an increase in pollution and resource depletion.
Although there is disagreement about the nature of the
problem, there is wide agreement among social and physical scientists that this hypothesis is correct. The
real theoretical problem appears to be whether or not
this process is reversible.

A different kind of hypothesis that is widely held among social scientists is the Urbanization-
Mental Illness Hypothesis. This states that as urbanization increases, rates of mental illness increases.
Indeed we find hospitalization and outpatients rates
increasing during the past thirty years.[122] The difficulty with this data is that it gives us prevalence rates
but not incidence rates. Many factors could account for
an increase in prevalence such as a greater tendency to
treat or commit nowadays. Even if we accept these prevalence rates at face value, there are other studies
which throw doubt on the hypothesis. A number of cross-
cultural studies fail to find a consistent relationship
between mental illness rates and urbanization.[123] Many
pre-literate folk societies have high rates of psychosis but some have low rates. Other studies conducted
in America have compared personality differences of
rural and urban people without finding any consistent
differences.[124] One historical longitudinal study, by
Goldhammer and Marshall, dealing with prevalence rates
in Massachusetts since 1840, found no increases among
people under fifty.[125] The increase in the older age
group was attributed to the earlier tendency of keeping
elder, senile people at home, whereas now they are more
likely to be institutionalized.

The evidence then, at present, is inconclu-
sive regarding this hypothesis.

Another hypothesis dealing with dysfunctions in urban society is the Urbanization-Family Breakdown Hypothesis. As the name implies, the hypothesis predicts that as urbanization increases, family breakdown occurs more often.[126] The evidence for this lies in the institutional changes that families undergo as a result of urbanization. We have discussed previously the shift from the extended family to the nuclear family structure as a result of urbanization. This is often cited as evidence of family breakdown.[127] Also institutional changes have made divorce easier and more acceptable as urbanization progressed. One result of this was a steady increase in the divorce rate in the United States since 1900.[128] This also is often cited as evidence of family breakdown. There is contrary evidence, however, to the hypothesis, such as the current high rate of remarriages, the highest rate of ever-marrieds in the United States' history, the highest average years of marriage, and a steadily declining age of first marriage.[129]

Evidence thus far makes it difficult to decide in a clear-cut way, for or against the hypothesis. We might be able to say, however, that urbanization in America has led to greater numbers of people being involved in marriage, but that the marriages may be less stable than formerly.

Alienation has been seen by many sociologists and others as a major dysfunction of urbanized societies. Although investigators disagree exactly what alienation is and what its individual and societal effects are, in general, it is seen as a negative and disrupting force.

Alienation has long been a subject of interest to sociologists and its relationship to urbanization has been debated extensively by them. A thread that runs through these discussions can be called the Urbanization-Alienation Hypothesis. This states that as urbanization increases alienation also increases. In fact, it is said that the history of western society since the Reformation, has been a history of man's increasing alienation from himself, from nature, from his occupation and from God.[130] Some of the foremost social thinkers of the past century have taken this position. Freud saw urban society (civilization) as increasingly resulting in man's alienation from his most basic instincts.[131] The alienation of modern man was fundamental to Marx's analysis of capitalism.[132] Durkheim's concept of anomie encompassed the dilemma of modern man

114

in a normless society.[133] Weber raised questions concerning the impact of bureaucracy and rationalization
on social integration.[134] Simmel, refers to the urban
forces which results in man's separation from himself
and others.[135]

It is little wonder that contemporary sociologists generally assume the validity of the hypothesis. There is hardly a voice in literature or science
that dosen't.

Again, we must say there is little empiri-
cal evidence to either support or reject the hypothesis.
A longitudinal analysis by Taviss, using content analysis of popular magazines concludes that self alienation
has increased significantly since 1900.[136] Other evidence, however, based on community surveys indicate
that less urbanized areas (in the United States) have
higher levels of alienation than large urban areas.[137]
These findings suggest, as Mizruchi has pointed out,
that it may be the change from folk to urban rather than
urbanism itself, that is alienating.[138] Obviously much
more work needs to be done in this area.

A final hypothesis concerning dysfunctions
of city life is Oscar Lewis' Culture of Poverty Hypothesis.[139] He asserts that in urbanized and stratified
societies poor people at the lowest rungs of the status
hierarchy develop a distinct (and somewhat dysfunctional) culture of poverty. He maintains that the culture
of poverty develops in all urbanized societies and has
a similar form throughout the world. The form it takes
is essentially dysfunctional for the people involved
and for the wider social system. Its characteristics
are negative from a middle-class point of view and include inability to delay gratification, violence, unstable social relations, isolation form the mainstream
social institutions, and distrust of authority. Critics
of this hypothesis center their criticism on the inadequacy of Lewis' data and his interpretation of it.[140]
At present it is a controversial and inadequately tested
hypothesis.

We have tried to present the various structure-functional approaches to the study of cities.
Whereas in previous sections of the book we dealt mainly
with the physical numbers and distributions, and characteristics of populations in urban areas. Here we have
ventured into the area of social organization. We have,
in this section, been interested in the ways that socio-

logists have looked at the social organization of cities, that is, the nature of social life in cities as it is expressed in institutions, social systems, role relationships, and other forms. The various structure functional approaches we have examined do not seem to be necessarily in conflict, but are in actuality alternative ways of looking at the same thing. For example, role analysis is the simplest and least abstract way of looking at the structure of the city. This is perhaps best suited to the analysis of small group relationships, but can also be extended to characterize interpersonal relations in the city in general. Social system analysis (including the analysis of power and class systems) is a somewhat more macroscopic and general view of the social organization of the city. This approach is perhaps most suited to the analysis of large scale organizations in the city, or the analysis of organized strata in the city. At the highest level of abstraction we have presented very general models which give some overall views of urbanized societies in general, (although they can also be used to look at particular cities). These very general models include mass society theory and institutional analysis.

F O O T N O T E S

[1]Norton Long, "The Local Community as an Ecology of Games," American Journal of Sociology, Vol. LXIV, (November, 1958), pp. 251-261.

[2]Talcott Parsons, The Social System (Glencoe, Illinois: The Free Press, 1951), p. 19.

[3]Ibid., pp. 58-67.

[4]Robert Redfield, "The Folk Society," American Journal of Sociology, 52 (January, 1947), op. cit.

[5]Ferdinand Tonnies, Community and Society-Gemeinshaft and Gesellschaft, Charles F. Loomis (edited and translated), (East Lansing, Michigan: Michigan State Press, 1957).
Emile Durkheim, The Division of Labor in Society (New York: The Free Press, 1933), pp. 70-132.
Charles Horton Cooley, Social Organization (New York: Scribner, 1909), pp. 23-28.
Sir Henry Maine, Ancient Law: Its Connection with The Early History of Society and Its Relations to Modern Ideas (New York: Holt, 1873).
Robert Redfield, o. cit.

[6]Emile Durkheim, op. cit., pp. 70-132.

[7]Talcott Parsons, The Social System, op. cit., p. 39.

[8]Robert O. Blood, Jr., The Family (New York: The Free Press, 1972), pp. 130-148.

[9]Talcott Parsons and Robert F. Bales, Family, Socialization and Interaction (Glencoe, Illinois: The Free Press, 1955), pp. 338-342.

[10]Robert O. Blood, Jr. and Donald M. Wolfe, Husbands and Wives: The Dynamics of Married Living (New York: The Free Press, 1960), see especially page 24.

[11]Kingsley Davis, "The Origin and Growth

of Urbanization in the World, "The American Journal of Sociology, 60, (March, 1955), p. 435.

[12]Ibid., p. 435.

[13]Daniel Bell, The Coming of Post-Industrial Society (New York: Basic Books, 1973).

[14]Talcott Parsons, Societies: Evolutionary and Comparative Perspectives, op. cit.

[15]Talcott Parsons, The Social System, op. cit., pp. 158-159.

[16]Robert Michaels, Political Parties, Eden Paul and Cedar Paul (translators) (Glencoe, Illinois: The Free Press, 1949).

[17]Talcott Parsons, The Social System, op. cit., pp. 158-159.

[18]Talcott Parsons, Societies: Evolutionary and Comparative Perspectives, op. cit., p. 22.

[19]Talcott Parsons, The Social System, op. cit., pp. 158-158. See also Durkheim, The Division of Labor in Society, op. cit., p. 138.

[20]Talcott Parsons, Societies: Evolutionary and Comparative Perspectives, op. cit., pp. 24-25.

[21]From Max Weber: Essays in Sociology, edited by H. H. Gerth and C. W. Mills (New York: Oxford University Press, 1946), pp. 294-299.

[22]Sir Henry Maine, Ancient Law: Its Connection with the Early History of Society and Its Relations to Modern Ideas, op. cit.

[23]Emile Durkheim, The Division of Labor in Society, op. cit., pp. 70-132.

[24]Max Weber: Essays in Sociology, op. cit., pp. 294-299.

[25]Herbert H. Hyman and Charles R. Wright, "Trends in Voluntary Association Membership of American Adults: Replication Based on Secondary Analysis of National Sample Surveys," American Sociological Review, 36:2 (April, 1971), pp. 191-206.

[26]H. R. Mahood, Pressure Groups in American Politics (New York: Charles Scribners and Sons, 1967).

[27]William Kornhauser, The Politics of Mass Society (Glencoe, Illinois: The Free Press, 1959), pp. 77-78.

[28]Talcott Parsons and Robert F. Bales, Family, Socialization and Interaction, op. cit., p. 35 and pp. 113-123.

[29]For a good discussion of role theory see the following: Role Theory: Concepts and Research, ed. by Bruce J. Biddle and Edwin J. Thomas (New York: John Wiley and Sons, Inc., 1966) Alvin L. Bertrand, Social Organization: A General Systems and Role Theory Perspective (Phyladelphia, Pennsylvania: F. A. Davis Company, 1972.)

[30]The Sociology of Georg Simmel, trs. and ed. by Kurt H. Wolff (New York: The Free Press, 1950), "The Metropolis and Mental Life," pp. 409-424. See also, Louis Wirth, "Urbanism As a Way of Life," The American Journal of Sociology, 44 (July, 1938), pp. 1-24.

[31]Emile Durkheim, Suicide, translated by John A. Spaulding and George Simpson, edited by George Simpson, (New York: The Free Press, 1951), pp. 246-254.

[32]Emile Durnkeim, The Division of Labor in Society op. cit., see especially p. 137 and pp. 353-373.

[33]The Sociology of Georg Simmel. op. cit. See especially pp. 411-413 and p. 422.

[34]Talcott Parsons, The Social System, op. CIT., p. 60.

[35]The Sociology of Georg Simmel, op. cit. See especially pp. 411 and 415.

[36]Ibid. See especially pp. 411 and 412.

[37]Talcott Parsons, The Social System, op. cit., p. 62.

[38]From Max Weber: Essays in Sociology, op. cit., p. 299.

[39]The Sociology of Georg Simmel, op. cit. See especially p. 415.

[40]Ibid. See especially p. 410 and pp. 412-413.

[41]Edward T. Hall, The Hidden Dimension (Garden City, New York: Anchor Books, Doubleday and Company, Inc., 1966), see especially Chapter 4.

[42]The Sociology of Georg Simmel, op. cit., p. 420.

[43]Talcott Parsons, The Social System, op. cit., p. 60.

[44]Martin Buber, I and Thou (New York: Charles Scribners and Sons, 1970), see especially First Part.

[45]The Sociology of Georg Simmel, op. cit. See especially p. 415.

[46]Ibid. See especially p. 411.

[47]Ibid., p. 420.

[48]The Marx-Engels Reader, edited by Robert C. Tucker (New York: W. W. Norton and Company, Inc., 1972), "Estranged Labour," pp. 56-67.

[49]Talcott Parsons, Societies: Evolutionary and Comparative Perspectives, op. cit., pp. 18-19.

[50]Neal Gross, Ward S. Mason, and Alexander W. McEachern, Explorations in Role Analysis: Studies of the School Superintendency Role (New York: Wiley and Company, 1958).

[51]Emile Durkheim, The Division of Labor in Society, op. cit., pp. 70-132.

[52]The Sociology of Georg Simmel, op. cit., pp. 420-421.

[53]Erving Goffman, The Presentation of Self in Everyday Life (Garden City, New York: Doubleday and Company, Inc., 1959), pp. 22-30.

[54]The Sociology of Georg Simmel, op. cit., pp. 420-421.

[55]Ibid., pp. 411-413.

[56]Ibid., p. 422.

[57]From Max Weber: Essays in Sociology, op. cit., p. 299.

[58]Floyd Hunter, Community Power Structure (Chappel Hill, North Carolina: The University of North Carolina Press, 1953), pp. 8-25, C. Wright Mills, The Power Elite (New York: Oxford University Press, 1956), pp. 3-29.

[59]Robert A. Dahl, Who Governs? (New Haven, Connecticut: Yale University Press, 1961), especially pp. 181-183.
Nelson W. Polsby, "Three Problems in the Analysis of Community Power, American Sociological Review, 24 (December, 1959), pp. 796-803. See also Nelson W. Polsby, Community Power and Political Theory, (New Haven, Connecticut: Yale University Press, 1963), especially pp. 112-121.

[60]The Marx-Engels Reader, op. cit., "The Communist Manifesto," pp. 335-362.

[61]Nelson W. Poslby, Community Power and Political Theory, op. cit., see especially pp. 122-138.

[62]From Max Weber: Essays in Sociology, op. cit., p. 187.

[63]Robert Redfield, "The Folk Society," American Journal of Sociology, 52 (January, 1947), op. cit.

[64]Stuart Adams, "Status Congruency As a Variable in Small Group Performance," Social Forces, 32 (1953), pp. 16-22. See also Gerhard E. Lenski, "Status Crystallization: A Non-Vertical Dimension of Social Status," American Sociological Review, 19 (August, 1954), pp. 405-413. Elton F. Jackson, "Status, Consistency and Symptoms of Stress," American Sociological Review, 27 (August, 1962), p. 476. Werner S. Landecker, "Class Crystallization and Class Consciousness," American Sociological Review, 28 (1963), pp. 219-229. Robert E. Mitchell, "Methodological Notes On A Theory of Status," Public Opinion Quarterly, 28 (Summer, 1964), pp. 315-325.

[65]Henry Pirenne, Medieval Cities (Princeton, New Jersey: Princeton University Press, 1948), see particularly pp. 161-167. See also Gideon Sjoberg, The Preindustrial City (Glencoe, Illinois: The Free Press,

121

1960), see especially pp. 118-123, pp. 221-22, and pp. 256-261.

[66] August B. Hollingshead, "Selected Characteristics of Classes in a Middle Western Community," American Sociological Review, 12, (1947), pp. 385-395, Harold Kaufman, "Prestige Class in a New York Rural Community," in Reinhard Bendix and Seymour Martin Lipset, Class, Status and Power (Glencoe, Illinois: The Free Press, 1953), pp. 190-203, Richard Centers, The Psychology of Social Classes (Princeton, New Jersey: Princeton University Press, 1949), Ruth Rosner Kornhauser, "The Warner Approach to Social Stratification," in Bendix and Lipset, Class, Status and Power (Glencoe, Illinois: The Free Press, 1953), pp. 224-255.

[67] Ibid., Richard Centers.

[68] From Max Weber: Essays in Sociology, op. cit., pp. 180-195.

[69] Ibid., p. 180.

[70] Bernard Barber, "Social Stratification: Introduction," in International Encyclopedia of the Social Sciences, Volume 15 (New York: The MacMillian Company, 1968), see especially pp. 290-291.

[71] The Max-Engels Reader, op. cit., "The German Ideology," p. 134.

[72] Ibid., pp. 136-137.

[73] Ibid., "Communistic Manifesto," pp. 335-345.

[74] Ibid., "The German Ideology," see especially p. 134.

[75] Ibid., "The Communistic Manifesto," p. 352.

[76] Kingsley Davis and Wilbert Moore, "Some Principles of Stratification," American Sociological Review, 10, (April, 1945), pp. 242-249.

[77] Natalie Rogoff, "Social Stratification in France and in the United States," American Journal of Sociology (1953), pp. 347-357.
Alex Inkeles, "Social Stratification and

Mobility in the Soviet Union, 1940-1950," <u>American Soci-</u>
<u>ological Review</u> (May, 1950), pp. 465-479.

[78]Talcott Parsons, "An Analytical Approach
to the Theory of Social Stratification," <u>American Journal</u>
<u>of Sociology</u>, (May, 1940).

[79]George Leland Back, <u>Economics: An Intro-</u>
<u>duction to Analysis and Policy</u> (Englewood Cliffs, New
Jersey: Prentice-Hall, Inc., 1966), pp. 338-350.

[80]Edward Shils, "The Theory of Mass Soci-
ety," Diogenes, 39, (Fall, 1962), reprinted in David W.
Minar and Scott Greer, editors, <u>The Concept of Communi-</u>
<u>ty: Readings With Interpretations</u> (Chicago, Illinois:
Aldine Publishing Company, 1969), pp. 298-316. See also
William Kornhauser, <u>The Politics of Mass Society</u>,
op. cit., for a general discussion of mass society see
<u>Mass Culture</u>, edited by Bernard Rosenberg, and David
Manning White (Glencoe, Illinois: .The Free Press, 1957).

[81]Arthur J. Vidich and Joseph Bensman,
<u>Small Town in Mass Society</u> (Princeton, New Jersey:
Princeton University Press, 1968), pp. 84-85.

[82]Melvin L. DeFleur, <u>Theories of Mass Com-</u>
<u>munication</u> (New York: David McKay Company, Inc., 1970),
see also
Leonard W. Doob, <u>Public Opinion and Pro-</u>
<u>paganda</u> (New York: Henry Holt and Company, 1948) see
especially pp. 423-529.

[83]John Kenneth Galbraith, <u>The New Indus-</u>
<u>trial State</u> (Boston, Massachusetts: Houghton Mifflin
Company, 1971), see especially pp. 25-26, and pp. 203-
207.

[84]William Kornhauser, <u>The Politics of Mass</u>
<u>Society</u> op. cit., see especially pp. 94-95 and p. 131.

[85]Elihu Katz, "The Two-Step Flow of Communication: An Up-to-Date Report on An Hypothesis,"
<u>Public Opinion Quarterly</u>, 21:1 (Spring, 1957), pp. 61-
78.

[86]Jacques Ellul, <u>The Technological Society</u>,
translated by John Wilkinson, (New York: Knopf, 1964).

[87]Eric Hoffer, <u>The True Believer</u> (New York:
Harper and Row Publishers, 1951), see especially pp. 29-

30, p. 36, and p. 49. See also
Orrin E. Klapp, Collective Search For
Identity (New York: Holt Rinehart and Winston, Inc.,
1969), especially pp. 63-70.

[88]Melvin L. DeFleur, Theories of Mass Com
munication, op. cit., pp. 140-142, and pp. 144-147.

[89]Arthur J. Vidich and Joseph Bensman,
Small Town in Mass Society, op. cit., see especially
pp. 82-86 and pp. 98-105.

[90]The Marx-Engels Reader, op. cit., "Estranged Labour," pp. 56-67, see also
Erich Fromm, The Sane Society (Greenwich,
Connecticut: Fawcett Publications, Inc., 1955), pp.
111-137.

[91]Emile Durkheim, The Division of Labor in
Society, op. cit.

[92]Bronislaw Malinowski, The Dynamics of
Culture Change (New Haven, Connecticut: Yale Universi-
ty Press, 1945).
A. R. Radcliffe-Brown, Structure and
Function in Primitive Society (Glencoe, Illinois: The
Free Press, 1952).

[93]Dennis H. Wrong, "The Oversocialized
Conception of Man in Modern Sociology," American Sociological Review, 26, (April, 1961), pp. 183-193.

[94]Amitai Etzioni, "Human Needs, Alienation and Authenticity," American Sociological Review,
30, (December, 1968), pp. 870-884.

[95]Talcott Parsons and Neil J. Smelser,
Economy and Society (New York: The Free Press, 1956),
pp. 19. Adapted from Working Papers in the Theory of
Action (1953).

[96]Talcott Parsons, Societies: Evolutionary and Comparative Perspectives, op. cit., p. 22.

[97]Charles Loomis and Zona K. Loomis, Modern
Social Theories: Selected American Writers (Princeton,
New Jersey: D. Van Nostrand Company, Inc., 1961),
pp. 72-85.

[98]Talcott Parsons, Societies: Evolution-

ary and Comparative Perspectives, op. cit., pp. 21-23.

[99]Robert K. Merton, Social Theory and Social Structure (New York: The Free Press, 1949), pp. 71-82.

[100]Ibid., pp. 60-66.

[101]Robert Redfield, "The Folk Society," American Journal of Sociology, op. cit.

[102]Emile Durkheim, The Division of Labor in Society, op. cit., pp. 63-69.

[103]Robert K. Merton, Social Theory and Social Structure, op. cit., p. 51 and p. 53.

[104]Ibid., p. 36.

[105]Norton White and Lucia White, The Intellectual and the City: From Thomas Jefferson to Frank L. Wright (Harvard University Press and M. I. T. Press, 1962) Chapter 15.

Carl. E. Schorski, "The Idea of the City in European Thought: Voltaire to Spengler," in The Historian and the City, editors Oscar Handlin and John Burchard, (The M. I. T. Press and Harvard University Press, 1963), p. 96.

Oswald Spengler, The Decline of the West (New York: Knopf, 1924).

Philip M. Hauser, "The Chaotic Society: Product of The Social Morphological Revolution," American Sociological Review, 34:1 (February, 1969), pp. 1-19.

Philip M. Hauser, "Man in the Urban Complex," unpublished, based on an extemporaneous talk at Loyola University Centennial Symposium, September 19, 1969.

Philip M. Hauser, "Whither Urban Society," unpublished manuscript, Highlights of an Address Given to The National League of Cities in San Diego, California, December 2, 1969.

[106]Louis Wirth, "Urbanism As a Way of Life," The American Journal of Sociology, Max Weber, "Some Consequences of Bureaucratization," Sociological Theory, editors Lewis Coser and Bernard Rosenberg (New York: MacMillian, 1957), pp. 442-443.

Emile Durkheim, The Division of Labor in Society, op. cit.

Sigmund Freud, *Civilization and Its Discontents*, translated and edited by James Strachey (New York: W. W. Norton and Company, Inc., 1961).

[107]*The Sociology of Georg Simmel*, op. cit., pp. 409-424.

[108]Sigmund Freud, op. cit.

[109]*The Marx-Engels Reader*, op. cit., "Estranged Labour," pp. 56-67 and "The Communist Manifesto," pp. 335-362.

[110]*From Max Weber: Essays in Sociology*, op. cit., p. 299.

[111]Emile Durkheim, *Suicide*, op. cit., pp. 246-254.

[112]Louis Wirth, "Urbanism as a Way of Life," *The American Journal of Sociology*, op. cit.
Emile Durkheim, *The Division of Labour in Society*, op. cit.
Sigmund Freud, *Civilization and Its Discontents*, op. cit.

[113]Philip M. Hauser, "The Chaotic Society: Product of the Social Morphological Revolution," *American Sociological Review*, op. cit.

[114]This view is frequently expressd by the mass media.

[115]The President's Commission of Law Enforcement and Administration of Justice, *The Challange of Crime in a Free Society*. (Washington, District of Columbia: United States Government Printing Office, 1967).

[116]Ibid.

[117]Ibid.

[118]Ibid.

[119]This view is also frequently expressed by the popular press.

[120]Hugh Davis Graham and Ted Robert Gurr, *Violence In America: Historical and Comparative Per-*

spectives, Volume 2, (Washington, District of Columbia: United States Government Printing Office, 1969), pp. 774-776.

[121]Barry Commoner, The Closing Circle: Nature, Man and Technology (New York: Bantam, 1972).

[122]For a full discussion of this see James H. Parker, "The Urbanization Mental Illness Hypothesis: A Critique," Journal of Human Relations, 20 (First and Second Quarters, 1972), pp. 190-195.

[123]N. J. Demerath, "Schizophrenia Among Primitives," in A. Rose (editor) Mental Health and Mental Disorder (New York: Norton and Company, 1955), pp. 215-222.

[124]C. A. McMahan, "Personality in the Urban Environment," in T. Lynn Smith and C. A. McMahan (editors), The Sociology of Urban Life (New York: Dryden Press, 1951), pp. 748-759, and
Gerald Gurin, Joseph Veroff and Sheila Feld, Americans View Their Mental Health (New York: Basic Books, 1960), see especially pp. 228-230.

[125]Herbert Goldhamer and A. Marshall, Psychosis and Civilization (Glencoe, Illinois: The Free Press, 1953).

[126]An example of this can be found in The Moynihan Report and the Politics of Controversy, Lee Rainwater and William Yancy, editors, (Cambridge, Massachusetts: M. I. T. Press, 1967).

[127]Lloyd Saxton, The Individual, Marriage and the Family, 2nd Edition, (Belmont, California: Wadsworth Publishing Company, Inc., 1972), see especially pp. 355-358.

[128]United States Bureau of the Census, The Statistical Abstract of the United States, 1969, Table 54, p. 47.

[129]Jesse Bernard, Remarriage (New York: Dryden Press, 1956),
United States Bureau of the Census, The Statistical Abstract of the United States, 1971, Table 39, p. 32 and 1969 and 1970, Table 76, p. 60,
United States Bureau of the Census, Current Population Reports, series, p. 29, No. 122.

[130] Sigmund Freud, Civilization and Its Discontents, op. cit.,
Erich Fromm, The Sane Society, op. cit.
The Marx-Engels Reader, op. cit.,
"Estranged Labour."
Karl Mannheim, Ideology and Utopia (New York: Harcourt, Brace and World, Inc., 1936).

[131] Sigmund Freud, op. cit.

[132] The Marx-Engels Reader, op. cit., see especially "Estranged Labour," pp. 56-67.

[133] Emile Durkheim, Suicide, op. cit., pp. 246-254.

[134] From Max Weber: Essays in Sociology, op. cit., pp. 196-244.

[135] The Sociology of Georg Simmel, op. cit., pp. 409-424.

[136] Irene Taviss, "Changes in the Form of Alienation: The 1900's versus the 1950's," American Sociological Review, 34:1 (February, 1969), pp. 46-57.

[137] Ephraim H. Mizruchi, "Romanticism, Urbanism and Small Town in Mass Society: An Exploratory Analysis," in Paul Meadows and Ephraim H. Mizruchi (editors), Urbanism, Urbanization, and Change: Comparative Perspectives, (Reading, Massachusetts: Addison-Wesley, 1969), pp. 243-251.
Lewis M. Killian and Charles M. Grigg, "Urbanism, Race and Anomia," American Journal of Sociology, 67, (May, 1962), pp. 661-665.
John D. Photiadis, "Social Integration of Businessman in Varied Size Communities," Social Forces, 46:2 (1967), pp. 229-236.

[138] Ephraim H. Mizrichi, op. cit.

[139] Oscar Lewis, La Vida (New York: Vintage Books, 1965).

[140] Charles A. Valentine, Culture and Poverty: Critique and Counter-Proposals (Chicago, Illinois: University of Chicago Press, 1968), pp. 63-67.

C H A P T E R   F I V E

The Social-Psychological Approach

C H A P T E R   F I V E

The Social-Psychological Approach

We have already reviewed some models of
urban social structure which suggest certain possible
effects on urban personality. Simmel, for example,
has given us a picture of lonely, overstimulated, competitive, superficial, and sometimes manipulative urban man.[1] Several critics, however, have pointed out
that this picture is perhaps more applicable to the
people in the disorganized portions of the inner city.[2]

The mass society model of urban structure,
which has been discussed, gives rise to a similar image
of urban man.[3] It presents a picture of "mass man"
pulled and handled by powerful groups, subject to the
manipulation of the mass media, and depersonalized by
a job in a mass production or bureaucratic organization.
In short, we have a picture of a "puppet" being manipulated and depersonalized by enormous and impersonal
social forces.[4]

Other theoretical formulations of urban
personality are very similar to the two models. Goffman, although not an urbanist, presents a picture of
people struggling to establish their credibility and
identity in a fluid, heterogeneous and competitive
society.[5] Every social encounter is problematic, and
contains the possibility of being discredited or de-
humanized. Possibly his book, Asylums,[6] presents the
most graphic picture of urban man's dilemma, where individuals attempt to reclaim a little self respect,
identity and acceptance from an essentially hostile environment. His other books and articles recapitulate
this theme of perpetual struggle for social and self
identity in a competitive and hostile world.

Other theorists follow these three models
quite closely, although they emphasize different facets
of the problem of urban personality.

Merton and Weber, both paint a picture of
the Bureaucratic Personality in modern urban life.[7]
More popularized versions of this theme can be found in

Whyte's The Organization Man,[8] and in Putney's and Yablonsky's work.[9] Merton, in particular, points out the
"over-conformity" character of the bureaucratic personality.[10] He does what he is told, according to the
rules, even if it makes no sense. He apparently likes
rules and structure and lives "by the book." He develops a "trained incapacity" to solve problems not
covered by the rules.[11] All situations must fit into
the pigeon holes of bureaucratic logic. Putney and Yablonsky extended this analysis to include the bureaucratic man's callousness toward human welfare and his
"robot-like" response to people. He is not a warm and
compassionate person, but rather a cold, calculating,
and rigid person.[12]

Reisman's well-known typology of inner-
directed, tradition-directed, and other-directed personality types delineate still another model for de-
lineating urban personality. Tradition-directed Personality is found mainly in folk societies and refers
to a personality directed mainly by a single tradition.
Inner-directed Personality is found in the early stages
of urbanization and industrialization and occurs when
a person internalizes group norms which govern his behaviour.[13] Other-directed Personality occurs in the
later stages of urbanization.[14]

Due to the complexity and fluidity of modern
urban life the individual's behaviour must be more flex-
ible. So the other-directed person is governed more by
the "situation" he finds himself in than by any single
group standard.

Reisman also sees a fourth type emerging at
the present time, which he calls the Autonomous Personality.[15] The autonomous personality is neither govemed
by internalized, rigid group norms, nor by situations.
He tends to orient himself according to personal standards which may be different from the situations and
groups he is involved with. Except for the autonomous
personality type, Reisman's typology shows the urban
individual gradually more estranged from his groups and
himself.

Marx saw increasing self and social estrangement as urbanization progressed.[16] The roots of urban
man's alienation, according to Marx, lie in man's relation to his work. In the latter stages of urbanization, the worker is increasingly denied control over
the "means of production." He can no longer do creative

and actualizing work. Without useful and meaningful work, man has no meaningful relationships to nature, his society, or to himself. Only when society is re-organized to give man back control over his work will alienation disappear. Marx saw alienation as the symptomatic disease of modern urban man and a fit des-cription of the root condition of modern life.

Since we have dealt extensively with Marx in other portions of the book, we will only extend his analysis here by giving a more positive aspect of Marx, insofar as he dealt with the individual, in industrial, urbanized societies. He did see the possibility of developing an industrial society (ruled by workers) which would give meaningful work back to men, and also give men control over their own destiny.

Durkheim expressed the problem in a similar way. For him the Malaise Moderne was anomie, or a breakdown in the normative structure of society.[17] This structural problem was due to the tremendous hete-rogeneity of values, roles, and cultures in urban soci-eties. Its end result was the production of the Anomic (alienated) Individual who has no definite standards or goals to guide himself with. According to Durkheim, when societal standards break down in modern societies, people suffer from lack of direction, goals and stand-ards by which to direct their own life with. The indi-vidual becomes cut-off from his society and as a result becomes alienated both from others and himself. Durk-heim traced the source of certain kinds of suicide to such a breakdown in normative standards. He also pointed out that modern, urban societies are more prone to the breakdown of social integration and as a result, a breakdown in individuals' personality systems. As we have pointed out before, Durkheim saw the source of so-cial integration to be different in urban-industrial societies, than in folk societies, and probably more prone to breakdown in urban-industrial societies.

Freud painted a similar picture of the Urban (civilized) Man.[18] He saw men who had lost con-tact with their fundamental feelings and instincts. They had, in effect, lost contact with themselves and were neurotic individuals with a thin veneer of civi-lization, who might erupt (or break down) at any time.

It is interesting to note how well the term alienation sums up these various descriptions of urban personality. Men as diverse as Marx and Freud, or

133

Durkheim and Simmel all see modern urban man as being
cut off from himself and/or his society. Euqally interesting is the lack of definite empirical work to
substantiate these claims. Although most intellectuals
see the modern dilemmas as alienation and urban personality as being alienated, little concrete evidence has
been provided to validate this perspective.

One root cause of urban alienation is suggested in the Meaning Breakdown Hypothesis. This hypothesis states that with the development of urbanization
there has been a gradual breakdown in the central meaning systems of Western society. The source of this
breakdown is unclear but some have suggested that it is
due to rapid social change and cultural heterogeneity.
Mannheim has most clearly set forth this hypothesis.[19]
He maintains that since the end of the middle ages there
has been a gradual erosion of traditional belief systems. Medieval theology suffered a blow with the Reformation and later developments during the Englighten-
ment. All ideas have become suspect and treated as
ideology. An ideology being a particular perspective
serving the interests of those that hold it. Several
events in Western thought served to weaken traditional
belief systems. The Copernican Revolution displaced
man from the center of the universe. Darwinism displaced man from his lofty position and made him just
another event in the evolution of the animal kingdom.
Marx introduced the class-determinism of social thought
in general and cast doubt on all political and social
thought systems.

Freud, through his emphasis on unconscious
motivation, raised serious doubts about the rationality
of man. In our own time Einstein demonstrated the re-
lativistic nature of conceptions of even the physical
world. Anthropologists were successful in promulgating
the idea of cultural relativism, which was taken to
mean by some, that one system of thought or behaviour
was equal to all others in value. Sociologists and
psychologists were accumulating evidence that we are
after all just a product of our cultural conditioning
or social environment. The deterministic bent of social science suggested that responsibility and culpa-
bility are social myths, and man had, after all, no
freedom.

Mannheim suggested that the only through
system to escape these traps was perhaps science itself,[20] but that was of only limited consolation.

Klapp has likewise concluded that urban society has resulted in the breakdown or trivializing of
symbol systems and that much urban mass behaviour can
be seen as a collective search for identity.[21] The
cults, the fads, the fashions, and crusades so evident
in mass society are ways that urban man uses to regain
a lost purpose and identity.

This all suggests that the urban problems
we face may be more at the symbolic level than at the
purely physical or organizational level. A breakdown in meaning, therefore, may underlie some urban alienation.

We have, in this section, been reviewing
the various theories concerning the effect of the city
on man, psychologically. We have looked at the ideas
of Simmel, Goffman, and others who all give us a somewhat grim and dismal view of the effect of the city on
man. Theorists as divergent as Freud, Durkheim, and
Marx tend to agree that urbanization and city life produce pathological effects including alienation, suicide,
breakdown in personality structure, and demoralization.
We might ask at this point whether the city and urbanization can be that negative in its effects on the human
psyche. Certainly most of the investigators cited here
are not basing their pessimism on hard empirical data,
but rather have tended to be theorizing with a minimum
of data. We might ask whether perhaps sociologists
have overlooked the positive effects of urban life on
the individual including, economic opportunity, opportunity for personality growth, exploration of various
facets of the self, and a wide variety of cultural resources available only in the city. We have earlier
criticized Simmel's rather pessimistic view of urban
role relations indicating that perhaps the negative side
of the picture has been overplayed. Certainly, more
hard empirical work should be done regarding the social
psychology of city life before we adopt, uncritically,
these pessimistic views.

This section of the book compliments the
previous sections, in that it suggests what the massing
of heterogeneous populations, together with the creation of complex social organization may do to the human
individual. It brings the problem of understanding
urbanism down to the individual, of his feelings, his
frustrations and his experience of life.

We will now turn to an approach to urban
sociology which fills out the major dimensions or ways

in which city life has been studied. We have begun in this book with the very general topic or approach of how city life began--a historical approach. We, then began to look at, perhaps, the least complex approach to urbanization and that was a study of population, whether from a demographic view, or a more sophisticated ecological approach. We went from there to the more complex concern with social organizations of the city, dealing with various structure-functional approaches. This provided not only a number of ways of looking at social structure, but also gave us some models that could take in entire urbanized societies as a frame of reference. We have just finished dealing with the social-psychological approach which presented ways of looking at the effect of cities on the individual. Now we will focus on the most intangible aspects of city life such as the values, goals, and beliefs that are characteristic of urban people. We have preferred to call this the Cultural Approach.

F O O T N O T E S

[1] *The Sociology of Georg Simmel*, translated and edited by Kurt H. Wolff (New York: The Free Press, 1950), pp. 409-424.

[2] Herbert J. Gans, "Urbanism and Suburbanism as Ways of Life: A Reevaluation of Definitions," from *Human Behavior and Social Processes*, edited by Arnold Rose, (Houghton Mifflin Company, 1962).

[3] Edwards Shils, "The Theory of Mass Society," *Diogenes*, op. cit.

[4] Erich Fromm, *The Sane Society*, op. cit., see also Philip Slater, *The Pursuit of Loneliness* (Boston, Massachusetts: Beacon Press, 1970) and Erich Fromm, *The Revolution of Hope: Toward a Humanized Technology* (New York: Bantam Books, 1968).

[5] Erving Goffman, *The Presentation of Self in Everyday Life*, op. cit.
Erving Goffman, *Encounters: Two Studies in the Sociology of Interaction* (Indianapolis, Indiana: The Bobbs-Merrill Company, Inc., 1961).
Erving Goffman, *Behavior in Public Places: Notes On the Social Organization of Gatherings* (New York: The Free Press, 1963).
Erving Goffman, *Interaction Rituals: Essays on Face-to-Face Behavior* (New York: Doubleday and Company, Inc., 1967.

[6] Erving Goffman, *Assylums: Essays on the Social Situation of Mental Patients and Other Inmates* (Chicago, Illinois: Aldine Publishers, 1961).

[7] Robert K. Merton, *Social Theory and Social Structure*, op. cit., pp. 195-206, and
From Max Weber: *Essays in Sociology*. op. cit., pp. 242-243.

[8] William H. Whyte, Jr., *The Organization Man* (New York: Simon and Schuster, 1956).

137

[9] Snell Putney, _The Conquest of Society_ (Belmont, California: Wadsworth Publishing Company, Inc., 1972).
     Lewis Yablonsky, _Robopaths_ (Baltimore, Maryland: Penguin Books, Inc., 1972).

[10] Robert K. Merton, _Social Theory and Social Structure_, op. cit., pp. 195-206.

[11] Ibid.

[12] Snell Putney, _The Conquest of Society_, op. cit., and
     Lewis Yablonsky, _Robopaths_, op. cit.

[13] David Reisman in collaboration with Reuel Denney and Nathan Glasser, _The Lonely Crowd_ (New Haven, Connecticut: Yale University Press, 1961), see especially pp. 112-114, 117-118.

[14] Ibid., p. 18.

[15] Ibid., Part III.

[16] _The Marx-Engels Reader_, op. cit., "Estranged Labour," pp. 56-67.

[17] Emile Durkheim, _Suicide_, op. cit., pp. 246-254.

[18] Sigmund Freud, _Civilization and Its Discontents_, op. cit.

[19] Karl Mannheim, _Ideology and Utopia_, op. cit.

[20] Ibid.

[21] Orrin E. Klapp, _Collective Search for Identity_, op. cit., see especially pp. 3-14.

C H A P T E R   S I X

The Cultural Approach

C H A P T E R   S I X

The Cultural Approach

Within City Differences

By cultural we mean the attitudes, beliefs, and values shared by a group, which are transmitted from generation to generation. Beliefs and values are difficult to measure in an urban setting, so we have decided to use Life-styles as indicators of underlying cultural modalities. It should be made clear that life styles are not aspects of culture as we have defined it. However, life styles are manifestations of underlying values, beliefs, and attitudes.

Life style is a concept originally used by Marx Weber to refer to the way of life or behaviour patterns characterizing different status groups.[1] We will use the term here in its original sense of being an attribute of status groups who share certain behavioural patterns.

Examples of the diversity of urban life styles can be found in such studies as The Hippie Trip,[2] Crestwood Heights,[3] Talley's Corner,[4] The Organization Man,[5] The Protestant Establishment,[6] and The Urban Villagers,[7] to cite just a few examples. Little work has been done in formalizing the relationship between urbanization and life styles, in spite of the enormous novelistic, journalistic, and scientific descriptions of this phenomenon. However, the literature does suggest to us some hypotheses which could be tested. It appears, for example, that with increasing urbanization, the number of different life styles increases.[8] Also we find that with increasing urbanization an individual is likely to adopt more different life styles both concurrently and consecutively.[9]

In effect, the urbanized individual may have multiple life styles and may experience a succession of life styles during his lifetime.

141

Also, with increasing urbanization there is likely to be a more rapid rate of change in life styles.[10] What was "in" yesterday, may be "out" tomorrow. Fads and fashion in life styles in urban areas are sometimes mentioned as being characteristic of mass societies.[11] These fads and fashions are not limited to clothing styles, but include popular arts, forms of address, fashionable social movements and changing values.

With increasing urbanization, a wider range of life styles emerge, encompassing most of what formerly was considered to be deviant behaviour. The drug culture, the swingers, the gay liberation people, are a few examples of this phenomena. The tendency, of labeled deviant behaviour, to become organized into life styles is very pervasive in highly urbanized societies.[12] All these tendencies exemplify the general thrust of urban "evolution" toward "differentiation" referred to at the outset of this book.[13] Other changes in life styles related to urbanization include a reduction in regional differences and a tendency toward national and even international life styles.[14] Obvious examples of the latter are the "international set," the worldwide "youth" style of life, and the spread of western clothing and music fashions.

The breaking down of traditional life styles boundaries due to urbanization is also evident in the declining role of social class and income in determining an individual's life style.[15] Within a given class and income range, a wide variety of life styles are adopted and often cross class lines. An example of this is the "hip-drug" juvenile life style which is distributed among all social classes and income levels.[16]

These general tendencies fit rather well into the mass society model referred to earlier. Life styles tend to be more widespread in mass society due to mass communication's mass movements, and mass production.

Mass communications disseminates to a wide audience the new fads and fashions which are often quickly adopted by millions of people. Mass production has the facilities to produce millions of products associated with these fads within a very short time. Mass media is often used to further promote the use and purchase of these new fashions through advertising and the content of the programs themselves. Mass movements through their extensive following, and usually very

committed following, can spread a new idea, fad or fashion very quickly, both within the movement itself and
outside in the wider society.[18]

          As might be expected, differences in life
styles between generations become greater as urbanization increases.[19] Urbanization, however, appears to
reduce the life styles differences between rural and
urban people.[20] This reduction can, in part, be traced
to pervasive influence of mass institutions and organizations. Again, the influences can be traced to the
mass media which reaches and affects rural as well as
urban people. Mass production produces the same products for the rural person as it does for the urbanite,
and mass movements reach into all parts of the society,
partly through the mass media, whether it be urban or
rural. In this way, everyone is subject to many of the
same influences, and a certain "sameness" in culture
invades all areas of the country, rural or urban.

          There also appears to be a reduction in the
long standing phenomenon of elite life styles "filtering
down" as urbanization becomes greater it appears to be
"warning." We might call this the Democratization of
Life Styles Hypothesis.[21] Under these conditions of
high urbanization new life styles appear to originate
at the lower or middle levels of society and "bubble
up" as often as they "filter down" from the elites.
Again this can perhaps be traced to the impact of mass
institutions. Clothing styles, language change, and
contemporary music are examples of this trend.[22]

          A good deal of misunderstanding about sub-
urban and inner city neighborhood life styles originate
from the lack of understanding of the basic trends we
have been discussing. The primary mistake with these
analyses was to treat suburbs and ghettos as homogeneous natural areas with similar life styles. This ignored important changes that were occuring as a result
of urbanization and other social forces which served to
generate many life styles in these two areas, which at
times, overlapped. We might call this theory of suburbs and ghettos the Homogeneity Theory of Natural
Areas.[23] Of course, the literature abounded with con-
tradictions to this theory, but sociologists were slow
to grasp their significance.[24] The fact is natural
areas are not homogeneous culturally or socially as a
general rule. An extension of this reasoning would lead
to the parallel conclusion that social areas contain
very diverse life styles and only in a very rough sense

could they be considered homogeneous with respect to a
few demographic variables.

It has become obvious that suburbs differ
from one another significantly. The primary difference,
perhaps is between the working class and middle class
suburbs.[25] Additionally we may distinguish between
the industrial and the "Bedroom" community. Within
these broad categories more subtle differences exist.
Some have an active social and friendship network,
others do not. Some are intensely political and divided, others are more cohesive. By dividing suburbs into
first, second, and third generations we generate still
another distinction. Each generation of suburban housing contains a somewhat different age group. The first
generation housing contains a large group of "young
marrieds" with small children. Second generation often
has a large proportion of middle aged people and third
generation housing often has large numbers of old people. Each of these age groups is likely to have a
somewhat different life style.

These differences between suburban communities can also be found within individual suburbs. We
find class, age, religious, and ethnic differences
within most suburbs. Added to this are the different
life styles found within the age, class and ethnic
categories. Striking differences have been found in
religious and social involvement, familism, and leisure
time activities, for example.

Inner city neighborhoods, are perhaps even
less homogeneous with respect to life style than suburbs. A number of studies indicate at least four distinct life styles in the Black community. These include the stable family (mainstream) pattern, the
street-corner men, the swingers, and the criminal adaptation.[26] Other styles include the religiously oriented people, the drug addicts, the musicians, and female-
headed households. Perhaps the most important distribution between these communities is the organized
and the disorganized "slum."[27]

Inner city neighborhoods also differ among
one another along the same dimensions outlined for suburbs, but especially tend to differ according to ethnic
composition.[28]

The proliferation and diversity of national
life styles mentioned earlier as a result of urbaniza-

tion, is found in both inner city and suburbs, with regional and ethnic differences becoming less important as cross national and national influences have taken over.

Between City Differences

Cultural differences between cities are harder to measure and characterize. Although one has the impression in going from Chicago to San Francisco, that real cultural differences exist, the sheer size and diversity of each city makes it difficult to make a comparison. Perhaps the best place to start is with Demographic characteristics since they constitute the most readily available data. The first variable we might want to consider is population size. Like most of the indices we will be discussing it measures cultural diversity. Here we may hypothesize that the larger the city, the greater the cultural diversity. This could be called the population size Cultural Diversity Hypothesis. Other indices measure essentially the same thing. For example, percent foreign born and percent non-white probably measure diversity. This Ethnic Size Hypothesis would predict that the greater the proportion of ethnics in the population, the greater the cultural diversity. If a large number of ethnic groups are represented in sizeable numbers, we would expect the cultural diversity to be even greater. The occupational distribution may also be indicative of diversity. A wide distribution of occupational categories probably indicates greater cultural diversity. This might be labeled the Occupational Distribution-Cultural Diversity Hypothesis. A look at the proportion of the labor force in various occupational categories (i.e., clerical, sales, professional and managerial, et cetera), might well give some indication of the predominant life styles and class level of the community. At the very least a city with a very high proportion of managers, officials, proprietors, and professionals would tend to be more middle class than a city with a high proportion of semi-skilled laborers.

Closely related to this index is the Functional Classification of Cities according to economic base activities.[29] Although cities are often difficult to classify it is clear that political, recreational, manufacturing and retail cities are sufficient of different occupational distribution to warrant some conclusions regarding cultural differences. Such an analysis would be based on the assumption that occupational differences generate differences in life styles and values. The sociology of occupations could well have some bearing on this general problem.

Other readily available data might also shed light on the problem of cultural differences between cities. Age distributions and sex rations are certainly variables to take into account. The high age distribution in Miami, Florida, and other resort and retirement centers are likely to have some bearing on the predominant cultural activities of the area. Sex ratio may well have some relationship to marital status, familism and perhaps sexual standards in so far as it is related to the availability of social or marital partners.

The class level and its attendant styles of life can be estimated form metropolitan area statistics which give income and educational averages. These bureau of census statistics also give data for each metropolitan area concerning services available in various cities. In particular data on health services is given in considerable detail.

Now that we have examined some of the cultural differences within cities and between cities it seems appropriate to spend some time examining another aspect of the cultural approach that is related to urbanization. That is the topic of the problem of cultural change and its relationship to urbanization and city life in general.

Cultural Approach

It is clear that there is considerable cultural differentiation within and between cities. Somewhat less clear, however, is the dynamics of <u>Cultural Change</u> as it is related to urbanization. In a sense we have been dealing with this general problem throughout the book. We have noted the aim toward complexity and differentiation in urban societies, and we have noted, in the mass society model, the tendency of large organizations, the mass media, and mass movements to initiate cultural change in urban societies.[30] We have also reviewed theories that relate changes in urban personality to social density, physical crowding, and bureaucratic (rational) organization.

Through a discussion of Parsons' pattern variables[31] it appears that some changes in role structure due to urbanization have occurred. Other theorists dealing with the Folk-Urban continuum have also noted these changes.[32] Such changes include universalistic norms, affectively neutral response, and greater specialization of roles. In other words, social relations come to be based more on laws or bureaucratic rules than on idiosyncratic personal relationships, people are more emotionally neutral toward each other in many relationships, and thousands (perhaps millions) of new roles are added to the social repertoire in urban societies. These changes appear to be related to the organizational response to dealing with large numbers of people, as in highly urbanized societies.

We have discussed institutional changes that are concomitant with urbanization. It is clear that greater differentiation of function occurs between institutions to "specialize" in certain functional problems more and certain institutions such as economic political, and military tend to grow at the expense of family and religious institutions. There is some clear relationship here to urbanization. As large numbers of people are involved (in cities), impersonal, rationalistic, and bureaucratic institutions such as economic institutions are better organized to handle the problems of organizing large populations.

Religions, and especially family institutions operate better with small groups and initiates face to face relations and are thus, of decreasing importance in many areas of mass society.

It is also clear that with increasing urbanization, there is a tendency for the rate of innovation and social change to increase.[33] There appears to be geometric progression in the rate of change with increases in urbanization. We might well call this the Urbanization-Social Change Hypothesis. There is also a tendency for technology to change the fastest.[34] Ogburn has incorporated this notion into his Cultural Lag Theory.[35] As he sees it, technological change outruns changes in other sections of society, thus creating a lag in non-technological areas. We are adding to this notion by suggesting that as urbanization increases, cultural lag may increase also. There are, however, numerous historical exceptions to this pattern. There has, in the past, been extensive urbanization without a corresponding change in technology.[36] Examples of

147

this may be found throughout the pre-industrial period. Also in many cases technological changes may precede urbanization and be one cause of it so we are dealing here with complex relationships between variables.

A final consideration here, is the interplay of Cultural Differentiation and Cultural Closure as it relates to urbanization. By cultural closure we mean the tendency of cultural strands or components to become unified and integrated over time, and to begin to form "wholes."[37] Differentiation is in a sense the opposite process of developing new forms and practices which are often at odds with existing practices. Here a general principle seems to suggest itself. This principle might be called the Closure Hypothesis. Stated simply, it asserts that with increased urbanization, differentiation occurs at the expense of closure, the likelihood of having a unified and integrated culture becomes increasingly difficult as urbanization proceeds.[38]

We have, in this section of the book, taken a look at the culture of the city as it is embodied in belief and value systems. Since it is difficult to directly measure such things we decided to look at "life style" of urbanites as an index of belief and value systems. In other words we wanted to see how life style is related to urbanization looking at "within city" differences and "between city" differences. Finally we took a look at cultural change in urbanized societies and settings. All of these three approaches pointed at a picture of rapidly changing life styles, proliferation of life styles, and a certain degree or homogeneization of life styles, where fads and fashions can be found in similar form in different areas of the country and in urban and rural areas.

This section and approach to the study of urban sociology is complimentary to the other approaches we have look at. It fills out our discussion of population variables and social structural approaches by introducing the whole area of value and belief systems as they are exemplified in differing life-styles. On the negative side, it is very difficult to measure such phenomena on a very wide scale, and requires many studies of different neighborhoods and different culture-groups within the city. On the positive side this approach does get down to the everyday modes of living and the whole problem of value and belief systems as they relate to urbanization. If this section has accom-

148

plished nothing else, it has show the wide diversity
of life styles, value systems, and belief systems in
our urban society. It, furthermore, has shown the dynamic way in which these things rapidly change.

This next approach is an expansion of our
earlier discussions of power and status systems where
the primary emphasis is upon <u>conflict</u> within the urban
community. Here we will try <u>to show</u> how such an approach has been used and its difficulties and advantages.

FOOTNOTES

[1]From Max Weber: Essays in Sociology,
edited by H. H. Gerth and C. W. Mills (New York: Oxford University Press, 1946), pp. 186-187.

[2]Lewis Yablonsky, The Hippie Trip (New
York: Western Publishing Company, Inc., 1968).

[3]John R. Seeley, R. Alexander Sim and
Elizabeth W. Loosley, Crestwood Heights: A study of
the Culture of Suburban Life (New York: John Wiley and
Sons, Inc., 1963).

[4]Elliot Liebow, Tally's Corner: A Study
of Negro Streetcorner Men, (Boston, Massachusetts:
Little, Brown and Company, 1967).

[5]William H. Whyte, Jr., The Organization
Man (New York: Simon and Schuster, 1956).

[6]E. Digby Baltzell, The Protestant Establishment: Aristocracy and Caste in America (New York:
Vintage Books, 1964).

[7]Herbert J. Gans, The Urban Villagers:
Group and Class in the Life of Italian-Americans (New
York: :The Free Press, 1962).

[8]Orrin E. Klapp, Collective Search For
Identity, (New York: Holt Rienhart and Winston, Inc.,
1969).

[9]Ibid.

[10]Ibid.

[11]Ibid.

[12]Edward Sagarin, Odd Man In (Chicago, Illinois: Quadrangle Books, 1969), pp. 17-31.

[13]Talcott Parsons, Societies: Evolutionary
and Comparative Perspectives (Englewood Cliffs, New
Jersey: Prentice Hall, Inc., 1966), p. 22.

[14]Orrin E. Klapp, Collective Search for Identity, op. cit.

[15]Gerard Lenski, The Religious Factor: A Sociological Study of Religion's Impact on Politics, Economics, and Family Life (Garden City, New York: Doubleday and Company, Inc., 1961), see especially pp. 8-12.

[16]Lewis Yablonsky, The Hippie Trip, op. cit.

[17]Edward Shils, "The Theory of Mass Society," Diogenes, 39, (Fall, 1962), reprinted in David W. Minar and Scott Greer, editors, The Concept of Community: Readings with Interpretations (Chicago, Illinois: Aldine Publishing Company, 1969).

[18]Orrin E. Klapp, Collective Serach for Identity, op. cit.

[19]Margaret Mead, Culture and Commitment (Garden City, New York: Doubleday and Company, Inc., 1970), pp. 65-97.

[20]Richard Dewey, "The Rural-Urban Continuum: Real but Relatively Unimportant," American Journal of Sociology, 56, (July, 1960), pp. 60-66.

[21]Orrin E. Klapp, Collective Search for Identity, op. cit.

[22]Ibid.

[23]Harvey Warren Zorbaugh, The Gold Coast and The Slum (Chicago, Illinois: The University of Chicago Press, 1929).

[24]Examples are: William Foote Whyte, Street Corner Society (Chicago, Illinois: The University of Chicago Press, 1943).
    Ulf Hannerz, Soulside (New York: Columbia University Press, 1969).
    Herbert J. Gans, The Urban Villagers, op. cit.
    Seeley, Sim, and Loosley, Crestwood Heights, op. cit.

[25]Bennett M. Berger, Working-Class Suburb (Berkeley and Los Angeles, California: University of California Press, 1969).

152

William M. Dobriner, <u>Class in Suburbia</u>
(Englewood Cliffs, New Jersey: Prentice-Hall, Inc.,
1963).

[26]Ulf Hannerz, <u>Soulside</u>, op. cit., pp. 34-
58.

[27]Gerald D. Suttles, <u>The Social Order of
the Slum: Ethnicity and Territory in the Inner City</u>
(Chicago, Illinois: The University of Chicago Press,
1968).
        Jane Jacobs, <u>The Death and Life of Great
American Cities</u> (New York: Vintage Books, 1961).

[28]Oscar Handlin, <u>The Newcomers: Negroes
and Puerto Ricans In A Changing Metropolis</u> (Garden
City, New York: Doubleday and Company, Inc., 1962).

[29]Grace M. Kneedler, "Functional Types of
Cities," <u>Public Management</u>, 27, (1945). pp. 197-203.

[30]John Kenneth Galbraith, <u>The New Indus-
trial State</u> (Boston, Massachusetts: Houghton Mifflin
Company, 1971).
        C. Wright Mills, <u>The Power Elite</u> (New
York: Oxford University Press, 1956).

        Orrin E. Klapp, <u>Collective Search For
Identity</u>, op. cit.

[31]Talcott Parsons, <u>The Social System</u> (Glencoe, Illinois: The Free Press, 1951), pp. 58-67.

[32]Ferdinand Tonnies, <u>Community and Society-
Gemeinschsft and Gesellschaft</u>, (East Lansing, Michigan:
Michigan State Press, 1957).
        Emile Durkheim, <u>The Division of Labor in
Society</u> (New York: The Free Press, 1933), pp. 70-132.
        Charles Horton Cooley, <u>Social Organiza-
tion</u> (New York: Scribner, 1909).
        Sir Henry Maine, <u>Ancient Law: Its Con-
nection with The Early History of Society and Its
Relation to Modern Ideas</u> (New York: Holt, 1873).
        Robert Redfield, "The Folk Society,"
<u>American Journal of Sociology</u>, 52 (January, 1947).

[33]William F. Ogburn, <u>Social Change</u> (New
York: Huebsch, 1922).

[34]Ibid.

153

[35]Ibid.

[36]Henry Pirenne, _Midieval Cities_ (Princeton, New Jersey: Princeton University Press, 1948)

[37]Melville J. Herskovits, _Cultural Dynamics_
(New York: Knopf, 1967), pp. 31-32.

[38]Talcott Parsons, _Societies: Evolutionary and Comparative Perspectives_, op. cit., p. 22.

CHAPTER   SEVEN

The Conflict Approach

C H A P T E R   S E V E N

The Conflict Approach

A perspective increasingly employed in sociology is a <u>Conflict Approach</u>. Urban sociology, in
particular, might gain from employing this perspective,
since a number of "urban problems" appear to involve a
significant amount of conflict.

The problem appears to be what kind of conflict model to employ. In our earlier discussion of
community power it became evident that there was considerable disagreement among social scientists as to
how power and "conflict" should be conceptualized and
explained. One of the approaches was a conflict model
as opposed to a pluralistic or an elitist model. The
conflict model we presented at that time was <u>Marxian
Theory of Class Conflict</u>.

This model, as the label implies, suggest
that most social conflict is a form of class conflict.
In this conflict an elite and a counter-elite struggle
for power. The group which controls the existing means
of production eventually wins the struggle.

The struggle in urbanized (and industrial-
ized) countries occurs between the capitalist elite and
the workers, according to this model. The class struggle preceding this one, occurred between the landed
aristrocacy and the new Bourgeoisie (capitalists).
Basic to this doctrine is the notion that conflict is
an <u>unavoidable and inherent part of the process of urbanization and industrialization</u>. Proponents of this
doctrine view urban social problems as a result of capitalism. A critique of this theory should be made at
this point. First of all it has been the underdeveloped,
less urbanized countries that have undergone the socia-
list revolution, not the most urbanized ones. Secondly,
class conflict has not become the primary type of conflict in urbanized countries, although it may be latent
in other conflicts. Finally, many studies of urban
communities have not found the basic power structure to
be organized in terms of class conflict.

Another conflict model, seldom employed explicitly by urban sociologists, is that developed by Freud and his followers.[1] The Freudian Theory is very similar to that of Thomas Hobbes, developed earlier. It poses a basic conflict between man's instinctual needs and repressive nature of culture and social organization. As urbanization (civilization) develops, man is increasingly forced to repress his instinctual needs. This repression and consequent neurosis in the individual grow more severe as civilization develops. The external conflicts between individual and society eventually results in internal conflict within the individual as he is forced to repress more and more of his experience. Conflict within the individual can then become externalized into social conflict with others. It seems clear that Freud was suggesting that more urbanization leads to greater social conflict and eventual societal breakdown. In general he saw the basic interests of the individual and society in conflict and this conflict was destructive and undesireable. The basic criticism of this approach assumes the interests of the society as a whole and the individual are different, and it ignores the fact that culture and society contributes to the growth and development (in a positive sense) of the individual. There are differences between societies and within societies with regard to the degree of conflict between societal and individual interests. An urban society, for example, may be very congenial and constructive for the upper or middle classes, and detrimental to the needs and interests of the lower classes. Also we might add that various ethnologies conducted by anthropologists find pre-urban societies which suppress individual needs to a greater extent than in some highly urbanized societies.

A third conflict model takes an entirely different view. Simmel's Theory sees conflict as a positive social process in many cases.[2] It creates ingroup solidarity, provides tension release, resolves problems, creates group identity, and sharpens and resolves differences. It appears that Simmel saw increase of conflict and competition as an outgrowth of urbanization but he did see this as altogether negative.[3] Perhaps of all three models Simmel's is the most widely used among urban sociologist.

The three theorists described above form a continuum of pessimism regarding the possibility of dealing with urban conflict. Freud is the most pessimistic in his dualism between individual and urban society.

Marx is perhaps in the middle, seeing conflict as a necessary historical, evolutionary and urban process, while Simmel at the positive end of the continuum, saw many positive attributes to conflict in urban studies. They all saw urbanization leading to more conflict.

These men and others have suggested numerous ways to "resolve urban conflict."

These Resolution of Conflicts state that some have suggested and actually developed cooperative rural communes where conflict was minimized. The Kibbutz movement is perhaps the best example of this.[4] Others advocate reducing conflict in urban societies introducing competitive systems such as capitalism and constitutional democracy. Still others have suggested the use of mediating mechanisms such as arbitration, mediation, and collective bargaining in conflict situations. In industrial urban societies, ethnic and racial conflict is often generated by social (urban) organization and institutional structure and must be dealt with by changing that structure.

Perhaps the epitome of this kind of "structural" thinking is anthropologist Ruth Benedict's idea of synergy.[5] A high synergic society is one where there is little conflict between self interest and social interest. By acting in one's own self interest, one automatically fulfills his societal obligations. These, in general, seem to be societies with cooperative social systems where one is rewarded for achieving group goals. At the other end of the scale are low-synergic societies which have direct and severe conflicts between self and social interests. Benedict considered American culture to be somewhere in the middle. The lesson to be learned here is that the structure of society is highly related to the amount of conflict in that society and that structural changes are needed in urban societies to change patterns of conflict to any great extent.

In direct opposition to the structural theory of conflict resolution is the Psychological Approach Model. As the title implies, this model seeks to change the individual's patterns of behavior and attitudes and virtually ignores its source in urban institutions. Conflict is seen in this model as a reflection of personality or emotional problems. Interpersonal conflict is often viewed as a result of conflict within the individual and if he could come to recognize and deal with

159

these conflicts, his social conflicts would diminish,
if not disappear. Therapy, then becomes the antidote
for social conflict on a small scale. Various thera-
pies exist for this purpose. Perhaps most widely known
is the conventional or traditional psychotherapy, Freudian or otherwise, where through talking with the thera-
pist, insight and behaviour change is supposed to occur.
More recently two other approaches are showing some
promise. One approach is the <u>encounter group</u> approach.[6]
The <u>encounter group model</u> varies from group to group,
but the basic approaoch is the same, this approach
tries to get people to talk and relate to others in a
group setting, where a climate of trust and acceptance
can be built up, hopefully, resulting in behaviour and
attitude change.

Behaviour modification is a third major
approach, stemming from the work of experimental psychologists. The <u>behaviour modification model</u> assumes
that if an appropriate reinforcement schedule can be
designed and applied to an individual's behaviour, behaviour patterns can be changed rather quickly.[7] For
example if a person has adverse responses to group
situations and tends to get into conflict with those
around him, the behaviour is altered by rewarding or
"reinforcing" smooth group involvement and ignoring or
perhaps punishing non acceptable behaviours.

In summary, the conflict approach is actually a number of different approaches, each of which attributes the source of conflict to different sources.
The one thing they have in common is that they all see
conflict in society as the primary social process.
They seek either the elimination of conflict or see conflict as a positive aspect of human and societal evolution. On the negative side this approach suffers
from lack of agreement on the causes, uses, and cures
of conflict. Conflict theorists disagree with each
other on many of these issues. On the positive side,
the conflict approach focuses attention on an important
social process (conflict) that no doubt shapes to a
great extent the form and function of urban communities.

Its integration with other theories we have
discussed is simply that conflict theory centers its
attention on one social process which other approaches
take into account but do not make paramount in their
explanation of urban life. The conflict approach differs from other theories we have discussed, in its
insistence that society is an arena of conflict and

dissention where groups and individuals are striving to overcome other groups and individuals. The structure-functional approach is perhaps at the opposite extreme in stressing the normative and functional integration of societies, and seeing conflict as a disruptive element in an otherwise balanced and cooperative system.

F O O T N O T E S

[1] Sigmund Freud, _An Outline of Psycho-Analysis_ (New York: W. W. Norton and Company, Inc., 1949).

[2] Georg Simmel, _Conflict_, translated by Kurt H. Wolff, (New York: The Free Press, 1955).

[3] Ibid., see especially pp. 57-85.

[4] Melford E. Spiro, _Kibbutz: Venture in Utopia_ (New York: Schocken Books, 1963).

[5] Abraham H. Maslow, _The Farther Reaches of Human Nature_ (New York: The Viking Press, 1971), pp. 199-211.

[6] Kurt W. Back, _Beyond Words: The Story of Sensitivity Training and the Encounter Group_ (Russell Sage Foundation, 1972).

[7] B. F. Skinner, _Science and Human Behavior_ (New York: MacMillan, 1953).

C H A P T E R   E I G H T

The Future City
(Planning Models)

C H A P T E R   E I G H T

The Future City
(Planning Models)

A further consideration in this book will
be the various models of how to improve the city and
how to build future cities. Most of the urban models
of the future seem to return to the problems of the
physical structure of cities, land use, and population
distribution. These are precisely the issues that concerned us at the beginning of this book.

The first model is the Laissez faire or
Organic Model. Proponents such as Jane Jacobs advocate
the minimum intervention into the "natural" growth of
the city.[1]

Her approach is to interfere as little as
possible in the natural growth of the city. She sees
massive government intervention as destructive in many
cases, and opts for mixed neighborhoods with many different activities and land uses. She is against the
kind of "zoning" which segregate activities and land
uses. The best criticism of this approach is that people vote with their feet, and millions of people vote
on this issue by fleeing to homogeneous suburbs and
studiously avoid mixed and multiple-use neighborhoods.
On the positive side it is clear that other people prefer these multiple-use neighborhoods and that government intervention is often destructive of sound neighborhoods.

The Limited Use Model adopted by most city
planners attempts to separate functions, such as residential, business, manufacturing and the like. This is
a particularly attractive model in a capitalistic society for zoning often corresponds with land values and
locations appropriate for each function. Because of
this, "zoning" is often a "post hoc" operation, where
areas are zoned after the "appropriate" use has been
established in practice.[2] The practical consequences
for zoning for limited use is to create homogeneous
areas, each having a specific land use. A criticism of
this approach is that it separates worker's residences

from their work and shoppers from their homes, necessitating much commuting. On the opposite side, zoning does protect homeowners and residential districts from noxious manufacturing processes and other uses.

Two other models include the High Density and Low Density Models, which alternatively advocate high and low population density. Most of Manhattan is an example of a high density model, characterized by high-rise buildings, relatively little open space and heavy traffic volume. The average suburb with its detached single family homes is an example of the low density model.[3]

An advantage of high density building is that it makes the maximum use of land. Its disadvantage is that there is an accumulation of traffic problems, parking problems, and sometimes, crime problems. On the other hand, low density building tends to "waste" land, often taking out of production valuable agricultural land. An advantage of the low density model is that it crowds people less, with less parking and traffic problems. It obviously gives people a little more elbow room and a plot of land they can call their own.

A partial resolution of these two approaches is the Garden City Model which combines high-rise buildings with a great deal of surrounding open space.[4] Obviously, low density housing is a relatively inefficient use of land and high density, a relatively efficient use of space. It is yet to be determined whether the "social costs" of high density building overweighs its advantages.

Several other models deal with renovating and relocating cities.

The Urban Renewal Model, in its various forms, seeks to rebuild whole areas of a city at once, especially run-down areas in the zone of transition. This approach assumes it is better to improve old cities than to build new ones.[5] The Urban Renewal concept has been criticized because it destroys the social structure and social relationships of sound and stable neighborhoods. It has also been criticized because it has tended to benefit businessmen and land speculators more that it benefits the original residents. In fact, the original residents are often in worse shape than before because the available housing at their price level has been reduced through the destruction of the old buildings.

The New Town Model approaches the problem
differently, in advocating the construction of whole
new cities, usually somewhat away from existing population centers.[6] This appraoch also attempts to pre-plan
the city in terms of efficiency, beauty and safety.
Often a balanced economic base is part of the pre-
planned structure. Often cities such as Reston are
built around one large center with subcenters arranged
around it. The large center houses more specialized
functions which require a large population base. The
small surrounding centers house less specialized and
more frequently used functions such as schools, grocery
stores, barber shops, and general retail stores. These
cities are often planned to reduce the need for auto-
mobiles, to allow for easy pedestrian access to facilities, and to have a degree of open space. Some of
these new town planners are working under the assumption that today's cities are unliveable and should be
replaced by new, smaller, pre-planned cities. Preplanning in some communities has gone to the extreme
of preplanning social systems as well as physical facilities. This is done, to some extent, by making
certain facilities available, such as court yards,
malls and swimming pools to facilitate friendly inter-
actions. Other planners have gone further toward preplanning governing bodies, associations, and special
interest groups.[7]

Somewhat newer in conception are Hostile
Environment Models which are mainly in the planning
stages. These include undersea communities, space
platforms, and moon bases.

These communities undoubtedly would be pre-
planned and scientifically constructed with both physical and social necessities in mind. They would, in a
sense, be packaged communities, with an artificial environment to furnish air, light, and other necessities.
It is hard to tell whether these dreams will become
actuality in the near future, however, space platforms
are already being constructed. It is too early to tell
whether these communities would be liveable and congenial to human beings aside from the technical problems involved. Perhaps the most frequent criticism
of such ideas is that we should spend our money improving existing cities and not waste money on under-
water and space platform schemes. On the positive side,
such developments would add to the habitable areas
where human beings could reside, thus increasing the
total habitable places for man to exist.

We will now turn to an examination of the practical consequences and practical usefulness of the theories and models presented in this book. Not all theories can be considered here, but some will be singled out for special analysis.

F O O T N O T E S

[1] Jane Jacobs, The Death and Life of Great American Cities, (New York: Vintage Books, 1961).

[2] Ibid., see especially pp. 6, 23, 84, 186, 192, and 226.

[3] Ibid.

[4] Ibid.

[5] Scott Greer, Urban Renewal and American Cities, (New York: The Bobbs-Merrill Company, Inc., 1965), pp. 13-34.
Jane Jacobs, The Death and Life of Great American Cities, op. cit., pp. 270-320.

[6] John Madge, "The New Towns Program in Britain," Journal of the American Institute of Planners, 28, (November, 1962), pp. 208-219.

[7] Leonard Broom and Philip Selznick, Sociology: A Text With Adapted Readings, Fifth Edition (New York: Harper and Row Publishers, 1973), p. 533.

C H A P T E R   N I N E

Application of Principles
to Urban Problems

Application of Principles
to Urban Problems

A real test of a good principles book is whether the principles can clarify everyday urban behaviour. In particular, they should be able to explicate the problems of people in cities and urban societies in general. Perhaps even more important, these principles should be able to organize and interrelate problems in a functional unity. It is not enough to take one problem at a time and cast about for "good" reasons for their existence. This "nuts and bolts" approach yields little understanding of the extreme interrelatedness of problems and the fact that they stem from many of the same properties of the social system and are governed by some of the same general principles. Just as the principles are interrelated so are the problems. Hopefully we can make the organization of the principles work for us, by applying this organization to the problems. We have found, for example, that the best way to conceptualize these principles is to see the main causal links going from macro to micro variables. We have found that if we start out with variables such as technology and population we can trace their effects on a second set of variables such as role. Roles in urban society, in turn, can be seen to have an effect on personality. This same approach can be used in the study of urban problems and their relation to principles. We will begin, therefore, by examining the macro variables as they effect or produce social problems, then tracing their effect to the level of role relations, and finally to personality variables. The cycle, of course, could be completed by doubling back and showing the effect of urban personality and urban role relations on the macro-institutional variables and resultant problems.

Social Systems Integration and Urban Problems

Many problems of urban society can be traced to poor integration between various systems. Here, social systems analysis can be used to explicate some basic problems. The various sub-systems within the city (or within urban society in general) are often poorly integrated. The output of one system often does not mesh with the input of another complimentary system. The economic system is often in conflict with the governmental or political system, with the result that political programs and policies are subverted by activities of businesses and commercial establishments. The educational system is often at variance with the economic system, where, students are being trained for jobs that don't exist. In many cities the integration between government agencies themselves is poor, resulting in a great deal of wasted effort. Land use is often determined by two sets of standards stemming from different systems, with government zoning laws dictating certain uses and business interests dictating other ones. The clear fact that the city is not a unified system and is made up of poorly integrated sub-systems underlies many of these problems. The solution, then, to many of the problems arising here is a better integration among the various sub-systems of the city, and perhaps making the city as a whole a true functional system, not just a patchwork of over-lapping and conflicting jurisdictions.

Urban Growth Patterns and Urban Problems

Urban growth and land use in American cities, is governed mainly by the market and economic interest, and only secondarily by governmental zoning ordinances. Even where such ordinances exist they are applied unevenly and inconsistently. Variances to these rules more often than not are also governed by economic interests who are able to put pressure on government officials. Given this fact, it is not surprising that our models of land use in Sociology is predicated on the economic decisions of buyers and sellers in large part. At the very most, zoning regulations are only secondary constraints on the distribution of population and land use, which often reflect more than they determine these patterns of land use. Given this fact, certain distributions of population and certain kinds of land use results have important effects in terms of social problems. One result is segregation of function and of populations. This segregation results in several unfortunate conditions. First, various ethnic groups and occupational groups are segregated giving rise to a host of problems that we are all aware of vis a vis segregation. City services, including schools and police protection, are unevenly distributed resulting in gross discrimination. Perhaps more important, this kind of segregation results in a breakdown in communication and understanding of other groups. At the very least a sense of community (over the whole city) is difficult to achieve under these conditions.

A more severe problem exists as a result of segregation of function. Since residence and work place is often separated, commuting from one to the other puts pressure on the transportation system. The separation of commercial establishments from work and residence puts a further strain on the transportation system. Some have suggested that this separation of work and residence has implications for the socialization of children and the relation between husband and wife.

Since the husband is away at work most of the day, the wife's role becomes altered to a socioemotional specialty in which she regulates the social activities of the household and provides a continuous thread of emotional support at home. The husband's role also becomes specialized to include mainly his task-function as breadwinner for the family. It has also been suggested that the absence of males during the day deprives children of male figures to emulate and learn from. They, in effect, grow up in a woman's world knowing little about the father's occupational world, and perhaps even less about the father himself. This, in turn, may have some effect on the personality formation of urban children. It has been suggested that male children are feminized as a result of living in a predominantly women's world.[1] Thus we have an example here of a theory dealing with urban problems which links macro variables with role and finally with personality.

Size and Urban Problems

As we have mentioned, with increased size of a city there is a consequent increase in heterogeneity of population, degree of specialization, and complexity. These consequences have a direct relationship with several urban problems. The root of the problem caused by these factors is the increase in complexity. There is such a variety of roles, rules and procedures in cities that integration of all these becomes difficult. Also, at the individual level a person may find it difficult to manage the variety of roles and role relationships that he has. The heterogeneity of roles and people that he encounters may have further effects on personality. A personality may develop which is other-directed toward the expectations of others and toward changing, fluid situations. The person, then, may become very "situationally" oriented and behave according to the demands of the situation rather than according to fundamental beliefs and convictions. The variety of kinds of people in a large city, also means that the individual will encounter others who do not share his belief system or his style of life. This may result in a weakening of traditional practices and a questioning of personal beliefs.[2]

The increasing complexity of the city also has implications for the overall functioning of social systems. With increased complexity, the possibility of dysfunctionality and malintegration increases also.

The increase in heterogeneity of the population may be responsible for the great amount of conflict in cities. Racial disorders and conflict clearly are a result of heterogeneity. The appearance of fighting juvenile gangs and resulting disorder has been traced to underlying ethnic competition and hostility. In other countries there is conflict between Protestants and Catholics and tribal groups. Feuds of Jews and Arabs can be traced to such a source. Heterogeneity and complexity, characterestic of large urban centers, then form the basis of many of our urban problems.

Social Class and Urban Problems

The analysis of social class with respect to urban problems reveals some underlying relationships. First, class differences within the city provide one basis for conflict, which is perhaps expressed most openly in union-management struggles. The schools are also plagued by social class differences. Allocation of funds for education are sometimes biased in favor of the upper and middle class, with these privileged classes getting more than their share. The lower class child as a result gets a poorer education. Many struggles in larger cities over educational practices stem from this inequality, with less privileged groups trying to get a greater share. The allocation of good roads, cultural centers, city services, and parklands also reflect class bias. In short, social class and class

interests are reflected throughout the urban scene.
Political struggles, in general, in cities may reflect
underlying class struggle. The current struggle between wealthy suburbs and poor inner city people for
access to tax money is clearly a political struggle
with overtones of class struggle.

Institutional Change and Urban Problems

Institutional analysis reveals that significant changes have occurred due to urbanization.
These changes in turn have a direct bearing on urban
problems. Changes in the family institution have occurred concurrently with an increase in delinquency,
an increase in the divorce rate, and a change in sexual
standards. Whether these are direct results of changes
in family structure is still open to investigation.
Economic institutions have become more bureaucratized,
larger and more specialized, as urbanization has progressed. Some have claimed that this has produced widespread worker alienation and a general dehumanization
of the work role. Whether this is true or not also
demands further investigation. With urbanization has
also occurred changes in the scope of government, educational institutions, and the military. These institutions have grown at the expense of "primary group"
insittutions, such as the family and religious groups.
In general, institutionally we have seen rapid growth
of secondary groups and a reduction in the scope of
primary groups. It has been suggested that this may
have wide implications for urban society, including
effects on social control, socialization, and social
participation.

Mass Society Model and Urban Problems

Closely related to institutional changes
due to urbanization is the emergence of mass society
and its implications for urban problems. We have discussed to some extent, already, these implications but
we might elaborate on them further at this point.
First, it has been implied by a number of theorists,
that various aspects of mass society are conductive to
greater alienation. Mass organization, mass production,
and mass politics are the clearest examples of this.
Faced with these forces, the average individual is likely to feel powerless. Mass media also may have an effect on alienation by contributing to a sense of mean-

inglessness. Faced with a steady stream of conflicting views, and over-burdened with information from the media, the individual may react with a sense of confusion. Several other aspects of mass society conceivably have an alienating effect of people in urban societies. Mass movemetns may call into question traditional practices and social structure, and in the process induce a sense of normlessness in the individual. Some have suggested that mass entertainment may confront individuals with confusing identity models contributing to self estrangement, and through increasing "spectator" involvement induce a sence of social isolation. These contentions, at this point, have not been proven as fact and continue to be only hypotheses for further investigation.

Perhaps most important are other alterations in the social structure that mass society implies or produces, that have implications for urban problems. Mass society apparently alters the structure of authority in urban societies, with legal-rational authority becoming much more important. Traditional and charismatic authority suffer a decline. It is possible that the "decline in respect for authority," in urban societies that is so often mentioned, might be traced to such a source. Related to this is the fact that mass societies show an increase in bureaucratic organization at the expense of collegial or other forms of social organization. Whether or not this has an effect on alienation has yet to be investigated. The fact that in mass societies, socialization occurs increasingly outside the family, in secondary groups, and in bureaucratic and formal organizational settings, may well have an effect on personality organization and in turn have implications for alienation and mental health. The instatility of belief systems, practices and social organization in general in mass societies may stem from the pivotal role in these matters of the mass media. The proliferation of fads, fashions, and changing belief systems can be traced to some extent to the pervasive influence of the mass media. The mass media, then tends to take over from tradition, the arbitration and organization of social beliefs and practices. Whether this instability of belief and social practice can be considered a social problem or not, is of course, debatable. In any case various critics of mass society have seen this "rootlessness" of modern man as a serious drawback to personal development.

Population Size and Urban Problems

The rapid increase in population size as a result of urbanization, clearly has important connections with problems defined as "urban." Size is clearly related to complexity of social organization. Doubling the size of the city government, for example, makes it a good deal more unwieldly, as does doubling the size of the schools, the number of cars, et cetera. In turn, any increase in complexity results in a greater chance of malfunctioning of the system, in much the same way that a complicated automobile is more subject to breakdown than a simpler one. Aside from this, an increase in the size of the population, bringing about all the problems already discussed which are associated with heterogeneity. An increase in population size and density also puts pressure on available resources such as land, water, and air. This being the case, problems of resource depletion and pollution are likely to increase with a larger population. Size may also have important implications for social control and community solidarity. With an increase in the size and density of an urban area, individuals are less likely to know all other individuals, or even a significant number of individuals in that community. Since informal social control is predicated on the existence of intimate face-to-face relations, it can no longer function as effectively in a city or community where such social relations are absent or minimal. For example, in a small town, each person is able to keep track of the activities of a large number of his fellow townspeople. He can furthermore, exercise informal control of their behaviour through gossip, ostracism and other such mechanisms. In a large city neighborhood, people cannot keep track of or regulate the activities of many people in this manner. Either he does not know these other people, or even if he does, his approval or disapproval may have little influence on the others' conduct. Some investigators have attributed the high crime rate in big cities to such a breakdown in social control.

Not unrelated to this is the general breakdown in community solidarity that sometimes occurs in large cities. Often there is little sense of "we-ness" in such communities with the result that social control breaks down and people experience a sense of isolation and estrangement from their neighbors.

Population Composition and Urban Problems

Related to size of population is the heterogeneity of population. These are necessarily connected, since any increase in size usually produces an increase in heterogeneity. Perhaps, the most important dimension of population is heterogeneity. The presence of different and sizeable racial and ethnic groups sets in motion processes which are intimately related to other urban problems. For example, ethnic and racial groups tend to (as Park pointed out) compete for available space and housing.[2] Sometimes this results in racial disturbances and acts of violence. Other times it creates ghettos which are cut off from other areas of the city. The presence of ghettos usually indicates a restriction of housing opportunities for that group. Such a restriction may result in block busting, invasion of new groups into new areas and its attendant ethnic conflicts.

Heterogeneity also produces problems in schools, with the police, and in the general proliferation of group conflict centering around differing group practices.

Spatial-Temporal Patterns and Urban Problems

Regardless of the reasons for spatial patterns that develop in cities, patterns develop with respect to land use which have important implications for certain urban problems. One particularly central pattern is the separation of residential areas from work areas and shopping areas, which we have already disucssed. Other patterns of importance are spatial-temporal patterns, which determine the flow of people throughout the city during the day and night, and during the week. During the day most of the adult male population commute from home to work and back again at about the same time during the day. This results in "rush hour" congestion, and a host of traffic problems in general. Somewhat less important is weekend traffic which results from the flow of people and cars from residences to recreation and entertainment centers. These temporal patterns of traffic flow obviously are related to spatial patterns insofar as people are separated from work and from cultural and recreational centers. Thus segregation of function in the city is clearly related to urban traffic problems.

Related to this is the tremendous waste of
energy resources resulting from these patterns. Should
people live next to their work, schools, cultural centers, and recreation centers, travelling would be much
less necessary and the strain on the energy resources
would be decreased significantly. This tremendous energy use, resulting from extensive commuting, also has
direct implications for air pollution. With shorter
distances between work, residence, and recreation centers, there would be less automobile traffic and significantly less air pollution resulting from it.

Location Theory and Urban Problems

As we have seen there are various theories
accounting for the location of cities. Regardless of
the theories applicable to any individual city, the
decision to locate a city in a given place has severe
implications for urban problems later on. Let us only
take three cases where this seems to be the situation.
New York City, apparently was located primarily because
of its nexus to water transportation. Not only did it
have an excellent sheltered harbor, but it also lay as-
tride the Hudson River which provide a link with up-
state New York and eventually to the Great Lakes and
the midwest. This accessibility to water, however,
later proved to be a decided disadvantage when the automobile and truck became the primary mode of transportation. Surrounded, as it was, by water, New York City
was confronted with problems of gigantic proportions
when it came to land transportation. The only access
to the various boroughs, was, of course, over or under
the water. Therefore, with much effort and expense
bridges and tunnels were constructed. Even now, however, the bridges and tunnels provide only limit-
ted access to various parts of the city.

The second case is Los Angeles. Among other reasons, one basis for the decision to locate Los
Angeles where it is was obviously for its position near
the sea (and the orient) and for its position relative
to the mountain ranges to the west. These mountain
ranges, however, provided a barrier to transportation
which in turn required a "break of bulk" and "cargo
storage and handling area" at the foot of these mountains. Little did the pioneers and city fathers forsee
that these very mountain ranges would be the basis for
the city's severest problem. This problem turned out
to be air pollution and the mountain ranges provided a

barrier to the flow of air which had nowhere else to go. This, of course, became a problem only after the widespread use of the internal combustion engine and the pollutants it generated.

The third case involves the entire east coast of the United States which forms a megalopolis which has been called "Boswash," (signifying that it extends from Boston to Washington, D. C.). Each of the urban centers in this belt were located essentially for the same reason as the location of New York City, namely, access to the sea and inland hinterlands to the north and west. The net result of the separate location decisions, however, could not have been foreseen by the original settlers. All they were doing, from their perspective, was building a new city. The collective result of these individual decisions was, however, the pattern of urban sprawl, congestion, and various forms of pollution that we now see.

Migration Patterns and Urban Problems

Related to the problem of city location is the re-location of people. Regardless of the specific theories accounting for the migrations of people during the past century, these migration patterns clearly have implications for urban problems in a very direct way. The primary motivation, in retrospect, for the vast movement of people from rural areas to cities during the past century would appear to be economic. With the rural labor force shrinking, the growing technology in urban centers provided alternative sources of employment. Aside from this, no doubt, the pattern of racial prejudice in rural areas (especially in the south) provided additional motivation to move north and west into urban areas. The net result of these movements was a mass influx of people into the cities of the north and west, with a large proportion of ethnic minorities among the migrants. Obviously these movements contributed to the increasing size (and its attendant problems) of northern cities, and an increase in the heterogeneity of these cities (with its attendant problems). Two characteristics of these migrants account for many of the problems created by such massive migration. One characteristic was the rural background of the migrant.

Some of the problems of the city stem from the patterns of behaviour of rural migrants, which are ill-adapted to urban culture. Noise levels, sanitary

184

practices, and educational levels that could be tole-
rated in a rural setting constitute serious problems
in an urban environment. Socialized in a gemeinschaft
society, the rural migrant is ill suited to dealing
with an impersonal, bureaucratic, and complex society.
The city is faced, then with the problem of re-social-
izing thousands (or millions) of these migrants to cope
with the emergencies of urban life. Another characteristic of migrants to the northern cities that creat problems for the migrants themselves and for the cities,
is their minority status. Many migrants during the
1940's and 1950's were Black, Puerto Rican, Indian, or
Mexican. In many cases the cultures of these people
were so different from the receiving culture, that radical alterations had to be made in the migrant's living patterns, language and culture before they could
be successfully assimilated or accommodated. Language
differences (even for Blacks) created an impediment for
advancement at work and at school. Work habits, sexual
mores, living patterns, and various styles of life had
to be changed before suitable accommodation could be
made. Therefore, a great amount of resources in the
northern cities had to be committed to a massive resocialization effort in the schools and in industry.
The adjustment, however, was not just one way, in terms
of the adjustment of migrants. The receiving populations themselves had to make adjustments to the different cultures and ways of life they were encountering.
In some cases this went smoothly but others resulted in
conflict, prejudice, and confusion. In any case, this
process of mutual accommodation and assimilation is
still going on and will no doubt continue.

Theories of Conflict and Urban Problems

          We have just indicated that some conflict
may come as a result of personal, cultural or social
characteristics of individuals and their lack of it.
We have also shown that some conflict within the city
can be explained on the basis of communication problems,
or lack of agreement on values among various groups.
These are the sources of conflict that Simmel or Freud
would be most interested in. There are other sources
of urban conflict, however, that stem from structural
or organizational sources. This is another way of saying that the patterns of interaction that have become
regularized or institutionalized can be sources of conflict in urban settings. The main theorist dealing

with this kind of conflict is Karl Marx, but of course, this perspective is not limited to Marx alone. There is a more general sociological perspective (including Marx) which looks at sources of conflict and strain in a society, as a result of the whole system of practices which reinforce one another. This is, of course, the perspective of "structural sociology." A bona fide structural sociology would have to come to the conclusion that conflict is built into the social structure of American society, and especially urban American society. These conflicts do not occur in spite of the social structure, but rather because of it. Furthermore, the structural sources of conflict are not latent and unanticipated, but in many cases, were self-consciously built into the system by the designers. Like Simmel, they (the designers) though that conflict within certain bounds was constructive and useful. To illustrate what we mean here, let us examine several institutions with respect to their development and functioning and see the centrality that conflict has in them. Let us take, first the American economic system, as it is in theory and practice. In theory, the American economic system is based on capitalism of a laissez faire variety. This system, summarized by Adam Smith in the 18th century, was built on conflict (or competition in its more virilent form). The system was set up to put firm against firm in a competitive struggle (actual conflict) and laborer against laborer. Out of this struggle, theoretically, the best use of resources would result, as well as the most efficient mode of production and distribution. As the system exists in practice it is watered down with various adaptations that reduce competition and conflict. These practices include unionization and collective bargaining, advertising and the creation of demand, and tactics such as collusion, monopoly and oligopolistic practices. Nevertheless, even as it exists in practice, capitalism creates and encourages destruction of firms, individual careers, and the putting of group against group. It is little wonder that the average worker and capitalist alike experience a sense of anxiety, as desire to overcome others and to dominate. The system, as it was self-consciously constructed and understood, guarantees this.

Let us take another institution to illustrate our point. This institution is political. The founding fathers self-consciously constructed a governmental system based on the balance of powers. The balance of powers in effect was a system of conflict, where each arm of government was forced to contend (i.e., overcome, struggle with) with each other arm of government. As the infrastructure of government developed (in response to this) in the form of political organization, the pattern was continued. Each political party was forced to struggle with (often in a fairly b r u t al way) and hopefully defeat the other party (parties). This kind of political struggle and conflict reached down to the local level where urban politics are rife with struggle, conflict, and dubious tactics. Clearly, urban government and politics has conflict built into it structurally.

A number of other institutions also have more or less consciously constructed to foster competition and conflict. In most educational institutions performance is measured by a competitive grading system, whereby only by defeating someone else can one get a high grade. This system reaches all the way through graduate school. Clearly, here again, we have competition and conflict built into a system.

Such a structuring of social relations in urban society is related to the amount of conflict that is generated. The only was to get rid of structural conflict is to change the structure, or introduce ameliorating mechanisms.

Power Systems and Urban Problems

As we have discussed previously, there are several different conceptualizations of community power structure, used by sociologists. The two main ones however, are the elitist and pluralistic theories. Whichever model is used, it is clear that power systems do exist in urban communities and in various ways contribute to the problems of these communities. The existence of any kind of power structure whether monolithic or pluralistic, presupposes a differential distribution of facilities, goods, and services. In other words, the basis of inequality, rests on an unequal distribution of power. Regardless of the model used by investigators of community power they have consistently found that higher status groups were more often in positions of power. These status groups might be mainly businessmen in some cases, or a combination of business and professional people in others. More often businessmen make up the bulk of those making up the power structure. This is true regardless of whether

the structure appears as an elitist one or a pluralistic one. Numerous other studies have already shown
that people in power in these communities use their power to benefit their own status groups. This again is
true whether or not it is pluralistic or elite in structure. The contribution of power structures to urban
problems under these conditions then becomes somewhat
clearer. We have, then generated a picture of power
structures, made up mainly of professionals and businessmen, using their power to benefit their own status
groups. If this is true then we might venture to say
that power structures in communities tend to support
programs which benefit the rich rather than the poor,
or which cater to special interests represented by their
status groups. The problem of poverty in all its rami-
fications then, may be aggrevated rather than amelio-
rated by urban power structures. The problems of poverty, of minority groups, and of the disadvantaged in
general may be shunted aside, while the problems of
special interest groups are focused upon. The degree
to which given power structures foster inequality varies from city to city. Also the degree to which certain interest groups control power systems and use
their particular advantage also varies. How the power
structure operates in a particular city to contribute
to urban problems can only be reconstructed through a
careful study of that city.

One additional problem may also be the result of the existence of power structures in cities.
That problem is outcome of power struggles themselves.
Often so much energy is spent in v y i n g for power,
the power structure has little time or inclination to
tackle the real problems of the city. Power then becomes an end in itself.

Complexity, Social Class, and Urban Problems

In other ways the poor may suffer because
of the structure of urban society. Here we would like
to show how the personality of the lower classes may be
adversely affected by the complexity and heterogeneity
of the city. We have already pointed out that greater
urbanization leads to a greater variety and heterogeneity of life sytles, ideologies, et cetera. These
structural characteristics may have a differential impact upon people within the city. What may be a positive characteristic of city life for one group of people may be negative for another different group of

people. In this case complexity and heterogeneity may be detrimental for poor, disadvantaged people, and self actualizing for advantaged or rich people. Faced with a variety of different practices, customs, organizations, roles and situations which demand frequent choice among alternatives, the poor or disadvantaged person may experience a sense of confusion and disorientation. This is especially true of newly arrived immigrants, very old or disabled people, and poorly educated individuals. When the choice of residence, of job, of associates, among other things demand a knowledge of alternatives and their consequences, such a variety of choice can be detrimental. The result is often bewilderment, confusion or an inability to act. To add to his difficulty, the poor or disadvantaged person does not have the time, energy, or money to take advantage of the cultural variety and opportunities for growth that a large city provides. What could have been an advantage is not a live option for the poor person. So we have a picture of a person who is bewildered and confused by city life, and even more sadly, cannot even take advantage of the opportunities that are there. His opportunity structure then is partly a result of his "ability to perceive and utilize" the available opportunities. To the extent that he cannot perceive or utilize these "opportunities," in effect, they do not exist for him.

The advantaged or affluent person is faced, in a large city, with some of the same opportunity structure. The free museums, concerts, night classes, and general variety of city life, is availabel to him also. But, he sees it, is able to take advantage of it, and does take advantage of it. One only has to attend these free concerts, museums, and night classes to find out that it is largely the advantaged who attend them, not the disadvantaged. Part of the reason he is able to take advantage of these opportunities is that he can afford to travel to them, hire baby-sitters, or pay the small(?) fee that is required. A free night class is not exactly free and often requires a fee of $35 to $40. This is a pittance for some with middle income or high, but for the poor person it is half a week's pay. Even going to the city zoo requires an outlay of several dollars for transportation, a few more for snacks at the zoo, and a suit of clothes that you are not ashamed to wear in public. Energy itself is required to take advantage of complexity and variety of a large city. It takes time and energy to plan a trip, to even conceptualize it, and to go there and return. Poor and

189

disadvantaged persons, for various reasons, often do not have even this much extra energy. The poor and the affluent differ to the extent that they can conceptualize the city with its opportunities, its dangers, and its unknowns. An unconceptualized or poorly conceptualized view of the city is frightening and forbidding, to the poor person. It is largely unknown and confusing. For the affluent, however, the city may be accurately conceptualized as to its opportunities (and dangers).

Perhaps more interesting is the defensive measures the poor and disadvantaged take against the complexity of the city. One common response of disadvantaged people to complexity is to reduce their physical, social, and psychological life space to dimensions that they can handle. This requires adaptations at several levels. At the physical level, the poor person often restricts his physical movements to his own house or his neighborhood for the most part. The rest of the world constitutes the unknown. Socially, he may also restrict his contacts to relatives and a few neighbors or friends. Psychologically he restricts himself to a simple model of the world involving few elaborations. His model(s) is adequate for dealing with his restricted social and physical world, however, when he is required to step beyond it, his model may prove to be inadequate. His restriction of life space works for him but it also works against him. It allows him to adjust to his limited situation, but it also prevents him from going beyond this life space and taking advantage of his potential opportunities that the city provides. Locked into this conceptual, social and psychological world, his world is restricted and the outer world (beyond his life space) is denied or ignored rather than explored.

To some extent the affluent person restricts his life space also in the city, but to a much less extent. He does take periodic ventures into the wider society, meets different people, and does new things. His life space has a flexibility that allows for these periodic explorations, thus enabling him to gradually enlarge his life space. In this way the complexity and variety of the city is gradually understood.

We are not implying, here, that all poor people react in these ways or that all affluent people take advantage of the city in the ways described. However, it does seem clear that the patterns just presented do exist, and provide differential adjustments and reactions to the complexity of city life.

Functional Analysis and Urban Problems

Functional analysis can be used at three different levels in the analysis of urban problems. The first level, examines the contribution of various sectors of the urban social system to the smooth running of that system. The emphasis is upon discovering the mainsprings of equilibrium in the system (or systems). For example we might look at the effect of co-op apartments, discount houses, or organized crime has upon the economy of the city. Do these factors contribute to system equilibrium or do they throw the system off balance and lead to dysfunctional results? We might also look at discrimination in housing, banking laws, and allocation of tax funds for transportation systems, and their effect on the urban economy.

The second level, examines <u>differential</u> functions of dysfunctions that various sectors of the urban social system might have. By differential we mean that certain structures, or practices, might be functional for one sub-system or collectivity but not for others. For example, we might look at tax laws favoring property owners, restrictive covenants in housing, or state laws regulating city government. We might also look at sales taxes and exise taxes and decide that they benefit the affluent but penalize the working man. Or we might look at the allocation of transporatation funds favoring highway construction and observe that this benefits suburban residents, the trucking and auto industries, but penalize the inner city resident who needs mass transit systems. Clearly a practice, institutional form, or system may be functional for some groups but not for others.

The third level, examines the structures, institutions and practices that benefit no one. They are superfluous and contribute little or nothing to either the system as a whole or to individual groups. On a trivial level the lecture system in universities or the sermon on Sunday morning are outmoded practices which originated when most people could not read or books were not available. On a more substantial level we have the outmoded social and political organization of the city where some cities are divided into hundreds (or even thousands) of separate political jurisdictions. Still another example would be the outdated building

codes regulating construction of houses which forbid
the use of new materials or modes of construction.

Technology and Urban Problems

The advent of technology and technological
change has brought many problems with it. Various urban problems can be traced to this source either directly or indirectly. A brief examination suggests a number
of relationships between technology and urban problems.
A more exhaustive analysis would uncover many others.

It is clear that modern technology is at
the base of most of our ecological problems. Air, water, and solid waste pollution can be traced directly
to this source. Likewise, the depletion of resources
is a result of advanced technology. It is also clear
that modern technology has changed work patterns and
work roles, in a way that may be disruptive to the society and the individual. Consumption patterns are also
altered by changing technology as it devises new products and marketing techniques. Changes in consumption
patterns results in changes in social structure (for
example, family interaction patterns) which are only
now being recognized. Perhaps the most important effect of rapidly changing technologies is their effect
on the rate of social change throughout the society.
Although no one has systematically traced these effects,
there is some evidence that technology is central to an
explanation of social change in modern societies.

Evolution and Urban Problems

The theories of urban evolution set us on
the right track for understanding the directions and
forms that urban civilizations have taken. They point
to some major structural trends in urban society over
the millennia such as increases in complexity, energy
consumption, role differentiation and population. What
these theories are suggesting is that as urban society
has developed societies have grown in population size,
increased in complexity and developed a high energy
technology. It is little wonder then that we find corresponding problems with the growth of urbanism of energy depletion, pollution, problems of malintegration
of social systems (due to their complexity) and population problems in terms of growth and heterogeneity. Implied in all these theories is a more general evolu-

tionary theory of change itself. As urbanization increased the rate of change increase almost geometrically. Change itself underlies and implies all these evolutionary trends. Failure to handle change constructively and let it get out of control, of course, is related to many of our urban problems. It is perhaps, the problem, underlying all others.

Role differentiation is a fourth evolutionary theory related to urbanization. It is our purpose, now to focus upon the dimension of role and its relationship to urban problems.

The Folk-Urban Continuum and Urban Roles

The folk-urban continuum provides a framework for analyzing urban roles and resulting urban problems. This continuum is essentially a statement about the way roles and relationships between people change as a result of urbanization.

Let us take one conceptualization of this continuum at a time, trace the changes in roles as a result of urbanization and see what relation these changes have to urban problems. The first conceptualization is that of Maine with its distinction between status and contract.[3] Maine states that society as it develops (toward urbanization) becomes more and more structured and organized through the use of contractual relations. No longer are relations mainly governed by status relations among individuals, but rather by legal "contracts" which state the required relationship in abstract and impersonal terms that are to be carried out. The individuals involved agree to this contractual relationship and it is enforced by the courts and other legal machinery. Usually, but not always, the contract involves a purely monetary exchange, with money being exchanged for goods and services. The result of this in terms of roles, is that relationships tend to be instrumental, cold and impersonal. Two people as whole persons no longer interact, but only aspects of those persons that is involved in the contract, which is usually very limited. When people in cities complain of the coldness and calculation of relations in the city, perhaps they are reacting to this very thing. When most of one's relations are contractual, one finds himself relating on a very limited basis to the other persons. Added to this, contractual realtions are often monetary realtions, reducing exchange and interaction to calculated interest in money and profit.

Another conceptualization of this continuum
is the mechanical-organic solidarity continuum set forth
by Durkheim.[4] Durkheim saw the source of social integration in urban societies as different from that in
folk societies. In folk societies the basis of cohesion was mechanical solidarity. Mechanical solidarity
means that people are cemented together in their relationships by ties of common belief and practice. In
urban societies, according to Durkheim, the basis of
integration is "organic solidarity." Organic solidarity is based upon the differences in roles that people
play not (as in mechanical solidarity) on similarity of
roles and beliefs. The real basis of organic solidarity is the complimentary and interdependence of roles
in urban society. Insofar as people must depend upon
others (in interlocking rolesets) solidarity comes about
because of this cooperation. This of course is a continuum and there is probably no case of pure organic or
mechanical solidarity. Most societies would have a
combination of the two. If it is true that the primary
glue that holds urban societies together is interlocking and mutually dependent roles, what implication does
this have for relations between people. Primarily, the
result may be that people do not share frames of reference and beliefs, thus be estranged from one another
even though they may be playing complimentary roles.
If people are continually involved in role relationships
with people who are much different from themselves,
with different beliefs, and interest, the result may be
to produce a social system where there are wide gulfs
between people and little sense of "oneness" or community. The city then comes to represent little islands
of belief and practice, and give people a feeling of
estrangement (alienation) from their fellows.

Cooley's distinction between primary group
relations and secondary group relations constitutes a
third statement of the folk-urban continuum.[5] In folk
societies role relations take place in primary groups.
These groups involve frequent face-to-face interaction,
and people tend to relate as whole persons not in segmental fashion. In urban societies people spend more
time in secondary groups which do not involve as much
face-to-face interaction and do not interact regularly.
Again, the implications of this for urban problems is
that people forced to relate to others in a segmental
way may react by feelings of loneliness and social isolation. Perhaps the sense of superficiality of rela-

tions in cities is a reflection of this. Somewhat similar is the distinction that Tonnies makes between gemeinschaft and gesellschaft communities.[6] Gemeinschaft refers to more of a primary group relationship and gesellschaft to a secondary group relationship. Urbanization clearly involves a move from gemeinschaft to gesellschaft community organization and roles.

Simmel outlines a set of urban role characteristics which are clearly different from roles in a folk society.[7]

Parsons' pattern variables can also constitute a dimension of the folk-urban continuum, and may help explain certain problems that new people to the city may experience.[8] Urban roles seem to emphasize (using Parsons' pattern variables) affective neutrality, universalistic rules, specificity of role requirements, achievement as a basis for role evaluation, and self orientation. This scheme may be useful in understanding newcomers to the city and their difficulty in adjusting to city life, particularly migrants coming from a folk or a small town society. If migrants come from folk societies they are likely to come with role expectations just the opposite from those just described. Instead of having a universalistic orientation the migrant is likely to operate on a very particularistic basis. Likewise, he is likely to be affective (emotionally expressive), in his role relations, and accustomed to being treated and evaluated according to ascriptive norms (who he is) rather than achievement criteria. Finally, he is likely to expect and feel comfortable with diffuse rules rather than specific ones, and will be more collectivity (group) oriented than self-oriented. In other words, all his role expectations will, in a sense be reversed and adapting to city role patterns, may involve a radical relearning process. His adjustment to the city, then, will involve a very significant resocialization in role relations. It is little wonder that migrants seem so slow in adapting to urban cultures, and usually end up living in colonies (ghettos) with members of their own groups.

Bureaucratic Roles and Urban Problems

Bureaucracy involves certain role prescriptions that have come to play an important role in urban societies. Not only do these roles play a large part in bureaucracies themselves, but come to permeate the entire social fabric of urban society. Max Weber has outlined (in his ideal typology) some of these peculiarities of bureaucratic roles. First of all the roles are affectively neutral, are guided by formal rules, and are limited to the technical problem at hand. Furthermore, they tend toward efficiency (in getting the job done) and instrumentality. They also involve a high degree of formality among the interactants with little focus upon establishing informal, personal relations. Impersonality is a key word here, since the bureaucratic role is almost a machine-like, non-emotional, non-attached involvement. There is little room for the intimacy and involvement of primary group relations.

No doubt the complaints of impersonality, non-involvement, and being treated like a number that we hear among city dwellers and urbanites in general can be partially traced to such a source. In other words bureaucracy and bureaucratic role-playing can be a source of alienation.

Bureaucracies also involve mountains of paper work, keeping of records, and mazeways of procedures. These characteristics may also contribute to urban problems. It means, for example, that the individual problem gets lost in the shuffle, the urgent problem takes a long time in getting attention, and great amounts of time and energy is wasted in just keeping records. Even beyond this, urban bureaucracies develop a rigidity and degree of cumbersomeness that makes it difficult to make changes. The bureaucracy often just does not respond quickly or creatively enough to new problems. These problems with bureaucracy affect all levels of urban society, but are perhaps seen with most cogency in urban government bureaucracies. One government official, for example, complained that his application for a model cities' program involved a pile of forms two feet high. Much of the inefficiency and lack of responsiveness of city government can be traced to these characteristics of bureaucratic machinery.

Life Styles and Urban Problems

Many new life styles are generated every year in large cities and in urban culture in general. Some die out, others maintain themselves for some time, and a few become a part of the ongoing cultural tradition. For example, the youth life-style, the Black Muslim life-style, the New Right life-style, are all recent life-styles spawned largely by city cultures. There are also many life-styles developed from special interest groups; such as groups with certain sexual needs, and groups with certain political beliefs. This melange of life-styles is one of the sources of diversity and vitality in city life, but it is also a source of a number of problems. One problem is the conflict between life-styles that occur in urban settings. The practices by one life-style often conflicts with, or offends, the adherents of another life-style. Just the existence of certain life-styles, such as the drug subculture, consititutes a problem for other groups opposed to it. Second, only to class conflict in cities, is the conflict between life styles.

A second problem produced by multiple life-styles in cities is the confusion created in people's mind concerning their own beliefs and practices. Faced with multiple definitions of reality, self, and the good life, many people find that their own traditional (or non-traditional) beliefs are being eroded or called into question. In short, a breakdown in conventional and traditional meaning systems may be both a cause and a result of multiple life styles.

Urban Personality and Urban Problems

We have traced the effect of urban social structure on roles and found a number of interesting relationships. Now we would like to trace the effect of urban roles on urban personality.

In our earlier review of the Urbanization-Mental Illness Hypothesis, we failed to find in the literature any clear-cut personality differences between rural and urban people. Nor were we able to find any convincing evidence that urban life resulted in an increase in conventional mental illness. This is rather curious in light of the volumes that have been written regarding the pernicious effects of urban living.

One possible explanation for these findings may be that we can no longer make distinctions between urban and rural living in the United States. To a great extent nearly all Americans are urbanized and subject

197

to the influences of urban society. Even the person living in a small town is influenced by mass institutions, enmeshed in bureaucracy, and subject to urban values. This is perhaps why we don't find any radical personality differences between rural and urban. If this is the case we can now focus upon the question of urban personality in general, regardless of where a person lives. We may, in effect, assume that most Americans will share elements of the urban personality. We may now study urban personality without being saddled with the pseudo-problem of rural-urban personality differences. Rather than looking for differences, we may now look for uniformities and sources in urban social structure of these uniformities. A number of social theorists have suggested certain directions that urban personality might take and in general there is a good deal of agreement among them. Although theorists focus on different aspects of urban personality, or different directions it migh take, there appears to be no radical conflict in their views. We might also keep in mind that folk societies have their own kinds of personality pathology, which arise from different sources. The picture that may emerge in the future might be that folk as well as urban societies generate personality pathology, albeit somewhat different in form and stemming from different sources.

It is interesting to note that all of these descriptions of urban personality have been rather inflattering images. The implication seems to be that city life disturbs and distorts human personality in ways that are dysfunctional to the persons themselves and the society as a whole. It is also implied that these distorted personalities are a result of social structure and role relations produced by social structure. The real question, it seems to be, is whether these personality types constitute a large part of the urban population or are only a small minority. Perhaps a more balanced picture would include the people (possible a majority) who successfully adapt to city life, experience personal growth because of it, and constructively contribute to the urban life that we are all so accustomed to.

F O O T N O T E S

[1] Patricia Sexton, _The Feminized Male_ (New York: Random House, 1971).

[2] Orrin E. Klapp, _Collective Search for Identity_, (New York: Holt Reinhart and Winston, Inc., 1969).

[3] Robert E. Park, Ernest W. Burgess, and Roderick D. McKenzie, _The City_ (Chicago, Illinois: University of Chicago Press, 1925).

[4] Sir Henry Maine, _Ancient Law: Its Connection With the Early History of Society and Its Relation to Modern Ideas_ (New York: Holt, 1873).

[5] Emile Durkheim, _The Division of Labor in Society_ (New York: The Free Press, 1933).

[6] Charles Horton Cooley, _Social Organization_ (New York: Scribner, 1909).

[7] Ferdinand Tonnies, _Community and Society-Gemeinschaft and Gesellschaft_, (East Lansing, Michigan: Michigan State Press, 1957).

[8] Georg Simmel, _The Sociology of Georg Simmel_, translated and edited by Kurt H. Wolff (New York: The Free Press, 1950), pp. 409-424.

[9] Talcott Parsons, _The Social System_ (Glencoe, Illinois: The Free Press, 1951), p. 19.

A P P E N D I X

A P P E N D I X

Theorists have suggested various relationships between urbanization and a large number of other variables. These relationships appear to fall into a fairly regular pattern which appears over and over again. The general thrust of the theoretical statements that seem to emerge was that large macro-variables are related to urbanization and in turn have an impact on the role structure of an urban society. Role structures in turn affect urban personality in a number of ways. Below we have outlined these relationships in schematic form:

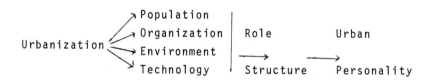

The second consideration is the format of macro variables. Here we find Duncan's[1] eco-system approach admirably suited to describe these variables. Duncan's POET Acronym includes Population, Organization, Environment, and Technology.

All of these factors are interrelated with each other and with urbanization.

A third consideration is that, although theorists have stated causal relationships are running from structural variables to social psychological variables, it is entirely probable that the causality also runs the other way. For example we might wish to alter the above diagram in the following way:

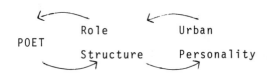

```
                    Role           Urban
        POET
                 Structure     Personality
```

Specifying these basic relationships even further, we might begin with the macro-variables, (e.g., POET).

Theorists have broken down these macro-variables roughly in the following way:

1. <u>Population</u>
   a. size
   b. growth
   c. movement
   d. density
   e. heterogeneity

2. <u>Organization</u>
   a. rationalization
   b. bureaucratization
   c. differentiation
   d. mass organization
   e. institutionalization
   f. systems

3. <u>Environment</u>
   a. resources
   b. topography
   c. space

4. <u>Technology</u>
   a. industrialization
   b. specialization
   c. energy conversion

Our next level of analysis, <u>role structure</u>, has been broken down into the following categories:

<u>Role</u>
   1. Role Differentiation
   2. Role Change
   3. Role Conflict
   4. Role Specialization
   5. Pattern Variables
   6. Folk Urban Continuum
   7. Role Formalization

8. Status Symbols
9. Status Inconsistency

Finally, urban personality has been analyzed by theorists into several component dimensions,
as follow:

Urban Personality
1. Alienation
2. Mental Illness
3. Personality Types
4. Personality Traits

Each of the sub-categories could be further
sub-divided, especially at the level of organization,
however, at this point this seems sufficient since further breakdowns can be found in the text.

Substantively, urban theory can be partially integrated around some common perspectives at this
point. These perspectives appear to be mass society
theory, institutional analysis, social systems analysis,
and the folk-urban continuum.

Mass society theory provides a broad macro-
perspective on social organization of urban societies
at the very highest level. It specifies the broad outlines of institutional and social system functioning,
and the way this changes as urbanization progresses.
It further sheds light on how societal functioning at
the highest level effects communities and other collectivities at lower levels in urban settings. Perhaps
even more importantly, it indicates how these collectivities are related to each other in urban societies.
Only broadly-based processes such as mass organization,
mass production, mass entertainment, et cetera, give us
explanatory power to explain urban phenomena and urban
change in particular at the highest level of abstraction. It further dramatizes the fact that in urban societies, societal wide processes determine in large part
the functioning of individual communities. The community in a sense, then, is no longer the relevant unit of
analysis for a full understanding of urban societies as
it is in the study of folk societies.

Institutional analysis is a specification
of mass society theory. Here we attempt to show how
urbanization causes radical changes in institutional
structure and functioning. It is a lower level of analysis than mass society theory but is nevertheless

important in outlining in concrete fashion how institutions function in a mass society. We find for example that such institutions as the family and religious institutions lose some of their functions while others such as political, legal, and military institutions widen their scope and differentiate their structures. We find also that in a mass society, institutions become more differentiated from one another and begin to specialize in certain areas. It becomes clear that these institutional changes are often the results of macroscopic characteristics of a mass society, not changes that can be explained by the nature of individual urban communities.

Social system analysis is a different way of "cutting" up urban mass society. In the same way as we have discussed institutions, social systems can be linked to characteristics of a mass society. We have documented, for example, the ways in which the development of urbanized mass society has altered status systems and power systems, to make them more differentiated and complex.

Perhaps systems analysis has been most fruitful when combined with functionalism. Here we have been able to analyze the sources and degrees of dysfunctionality of the urban social systems. We have been able to examine a number of hypotheses such as urban decline, crime, mental illness, and alienation from such a perspective. Here we have been asking the question of how mass society may generate disequilibrium in urban social systems, and personal disorganization among the members of the society. Alienation, then becomes an index of dysfunctions in the functioning of the entire society, crime becomes an index of breakdown in social control systems, and the ecological crisis an index of the breakdown of "adaptive" systems. These breakdowns, moreover, have been seen as primarily a result of society-wide, mass-processes, and thus can be linked up with the mass society model.

Moving to a somewhat less abstract level of analysis, we can then begin to link changes in these macro-systems (e.g., mass society, social systems, and institutions) to everyday role enactment as it occurs in urban societies. Here we conceive of the concept of role as the link between social structure and personality. We have shown how these larger structures in urban societies alter the role structure which consequently has widespread implication for the development of urban personality.

A brief example of such a relationship, (e.g., between role and urban personality) is found in Simmel's discussion of role relationships in the metropolis and their presumed effects on the personality structure of urban people. Other theorists were discussed who carry out the same type of analysis. We have discussed theories linking anonymity of relationships with personal loneliness, rational calculation with suspicion, and frequency of interaction with nervous innervation. Regardless of the validity of these claims, the mode of analysis carried out by most of these theorists is the same. In all cases they attempt to link up role with personality structure. Some of these theorists even attempt to link up the larger structures in society (e.g., capitalism, mass society, et cetera) with personality structure.

The Pattern Variables appear to be useful means of organizing urban role characteristics, where we can begin to describe urban roles as being affectively neutral, universalistic, et cetera. The pattern variables, then summerize the various statements by other theorists concerning urban role structure and constitute a useful pivotal point for analyzing urban roles. This should not be taken to mean, however, that the pattern variables exhaust the possible descriptions of urban roles. It is clear that they do not and that the pattern variables must be supplemented by additional dimensions of role.

F O O T N O T E

[1]Otis Dudley Duncan, "Human Ecology and Population Studies," in Philip Hauser and Otis Dudley Duncan, eds., <u>The Study of Population</u> (1959), pp. 681-84.

ABOUT THE AUTHOR

Dr. James Hill Parker is currently Professor and Chairman of the Anthropology and Sociology Departments at Long Island University, Brooklyn Center. A native of Auburn, Maine, he received his Ph. D. in Sociology from the University of Iowa in 1965. He is the author of 27 professional articles, including articles in Social Forces, Sociology and Social Research, Human Organization, and The New York Times. He has just completed two other books; one, a 24-year study of Ethnic Identity of French-Americans, and a second on "Social Games in Conversations and Small Groups."